Eating an Artichoke

A Mother's Perspective on Asperger Syndrome

Echo R. Fling

Foreword by Tony Attwood

Jessica Kingsley Publishers
London and Philadelphia

With thanks to Columbia Tristar Motion Picture Group for the use of excerpts from the feature film *Short Circuit*.

First published in the United Kingdom in 2000 by
Jessica Kingsley Publishers Ltd,
116 Pentonville Road, London
N1 9JB, England
and
325 Chestnut Street,
Philadelphia PA 19106, USA.
www.jkp.com

Second impression 2000

© Copyright 2000 Echo R. Fling

Library of Congress Cataloging in Publication Data
Fling, Echo. R.
Eating an artichoke : a mother's perspective on
Asperger's syndrome / Echo R. Fling.
p.   cm.
Includes bibliographical references.
ISBN 1 85302 711 1 (pbk. : alk. paper)
1. Asperger's syndrome. I. Title.
RC553.A88F58 1999   99-43199
618.92'8982--dc21   CIP

British Library Cataloguing in Publication Data
Fling, Echo R.
Eating an artichoke : a mother's perspective on Asperger's syndrome
1. Fling, Echo 2. Asperger's syndome - Popular works
I. Title
616.8'982

ISBN 1 85302 711 1

Printed and Bound in Great Britain by
Athenaeum Press, Gateshead, Tyne and Wear

Eating an Artichoke

of related interest

Asperger's Syndrome
A Guide for Parents and Professionals
Tony Attwood
ISBN 1 85302 577 1

Pretending to be Normal
Living with Asperger's Syndrome
Liane Holliday-Willey
ISBN 1 85302 749 9

For Jimmy, whose courage and bravery
continues to astonish me each and every day

Contents

Foreword

Echo began her discovery of her son's diagnosis of Asperger Syndrome when his preschool teacher uttered the ominous words 'I think I need to tell you that I feel something isn't right with your son and you may want to consider having Jimmy evaluated by a specialist'. He was distinctly unusual in his ability to understand and play cooperatively with his peers; conversations included obscure extracts from his favourite movie, an irresistible determination to acquire all the specimens of his special interest and an acute sensitivity to particular sounds. Finding a specialist who could explain this unusual profile of abilities was not a simple task and this book enables the reader to accompany Echo as she discovers her son's perception of his world and other people's perception of her son.

Echo and her family are very brave in allowing others into their personal thoughts, feelings and experiences but her purpose is to share the knowledge she has acquired. At present, the greatest knowledge base on Asperger Syndrome is not in academic texts or easily accessible clinical expertise but dispersed among families. This book will provide parents with an affirmation of their experiences while professionals and parents will gain new insights into Asperger Syndrome and learn some creative strategies to acquire specific skills. Mothers of such children have developed abilities in understanding and translating their child's perspective to educate their family, teachers, therapists, other children and the general public. They have developed negotiation and diplomacy skills in managing potential conflict with government agencies, professionals and members of their family that are the equal of United Nations diplomats. Their commitment to the welfare and happiness of their child, determination to establish appropriate services, and fortitude in the face of rhetoric and ignorance must be acknowledged and steps taken to ease their situation. Echo also describes new areas of concern such as the impact on siblings of having a brother or sister with Asperger Syndrome and the politics of diagnosis and service development.

The title of the book refers to an artichoke of which she and others 'have to peel back the thorny layers to get to the heart of what's truly the issue with him'. Her conclusion is 'there are many lovely things about Jimmy's 'Aspergerish' personality that I find I value'. Her biography of Jimmy will be a tribute to his courage and bravery and of great value to fellow parents and professionals who seek an understanding of Asperger Syndrome.

Tony Attwood
October 1999

Preface

When the idea came to me to write this book, I approached my son Jimmy with my thoughts about making our story public. I remember chatting with him about the project at a local Burger King, which was our regular Wednesday night hangout during his sister's piano lessons. As Jimmy and I discussed the various aspects of the book, we weighed up the pros and cons of such a project. We agreed that the bottom line was to help others learn about Asperger Syndrome through our story. What was Jimmy's final word on the subject? '...And we shall help them – every one.' Dickens' Tiny Tim couldn't have said it better.

I wrote this book for several reasons, some of them purely selfish. The idea of keeping a family history is very important to me and this book serves as a record of five years in the life of our family. I also wanted an account so my adult children could someday learn of their mother's thoughts and feelings as she struggled to find answers as she raised her children. Research has shown that genetics play an important part in Asperger Syndrome. The chances are quite likely that my own children will be parents to a child with this disorder. Any voice of experience will help them. I also wrote this book for Jimmy. Historians always say that to best determine our future, we must learn from our past. When he is old enough to understand, it is my hope that my son will read the words I've written, with an eye towards better understanding the essence of his soul.

This book is not meant to be the end-all on the subject of raising children with Asperger Syndrome. I am not an expert. What lies in its pages is the story of one mother's struggle to cope. My initiation into the 'artichoke sisterhood' may not be the same experience as another mother's. What I hope to be of value are the shared experiences that all parents of children with AS hold in common. Compassion only comes through knowledge and understanding. If only one person is helped by the stories contained within these pages, the effort will have been well worth it.

Echo R. Fling
April 27, 1999

Acknowledgements

A deep thank you to my beloved husband and best friend Jim, for his good humor, his love, and his continued patience when the 'A-word' is brought up at social gatherings; and to my children: Jimmy, for agreeing to let me tell his story, and Caroline, who encouraged me throughout this book project in her own small way. Much appreciation to my sister Dina Roberson, for her unique and valuable insight as she read through my manuscript, and to my dear friend and mentor Pamela Tanguay, who was the 'other half of my brain' throughout this project. I thank her for the many brainstorming sessions, her listening skills, and her judicious use of a razor-sharp editing hacksaw. Thanks to Barb Kirby, for being there first – and always; to Robin Levinson for giving me the confidence I needed to begin this book project, and to Tony Attwood for not only supporting me in my efforts, but the whole AS community as well. Thanks to Jessica Kingsley for recognizing the need for this genre of books and for being a pleasure to work with. A debt of gratitude to Debbie Dono, Deanie Yasner and all the professionals who have given their efforts and hearts to our family. And last, I would like to recognize my parents, Marv and Doris Roberson, who by their example taught me perception, discernment, the power of prayer, and the value of listening to that 'still small voice'.

1

There's Something Wrong
With Your Son

'Come in, Mrs. Fling,' said my son's preschool teacher, gesturing towards the table with one grown-up sized chair and several tiny chairs. I paused. It's the old 'Goldilocks' thing again. I have never been able to go to a parent–teacher conference and find a chair that was 'just right'. Why are the parents always the ones that are made to sit with their knees up to their shoulders? I choose a tiny wooden chair and gingerly let myself down, hoping all the while that the chair won't break under my weight.

Mrs. Wood and I talk amiably about our harried schedules. I look around the brightly decorated room and notice one of the walls is filled with red apples, each with a student's name printed neatly on it. I quickly spot Jimmy's. During my chit-chat with Mrs. Wood, she spoke of her daughter, now in middle school, who was going through the typical pre-teen adjustment period. I talked of my father-in-law, who had been bravely battling cancer and was back in the hospital again. As we engaged in our polite perfunctory conversation, I notice Mrs. Wood seems a bit distracted as she arranges the folders on the table. Then suddenly she gets up to shut the classroom door. In the two years that I have been coming to the school for conferences, no teacher has ever shut the door during a meeting. My senses are alerted. Either something is up, or else this teacher is very formal. As Mrs. Wood walks back to the table, my maternal antennae are up.

It was November 15, 1991, the start of the third year for Jimmy at his preschool. At age three, we enrolled him with some of the neighborhood kids in a class. He had trouble socializing with his classmates so at age four we decided to have him repeat the three-year-old class. With his birthday falling in August, I figured this strategy would give him an extra year to mature before sending him to Kindergarten. Since boys typically lag behind girls socially, my husband Jim and I weren't too worried. In our view, Jimmy was just a little immature. Nothing would be gained by pushing him to go to school and we had nothing to lose if we waited an extra year. Most of our friends with boys who had late birthdays were waiting, we would too.

Mrs. Wood opens up a folder, which signals the start of our conference.

'Mrs. Fling,' she says with a tone of voice I hadn't heard before. Clearly this woman was under some stress. I waited and watched as her complexion quickly become mottled as she struggled with her words.

'I have been in this business for many years and based on my experience, I think I need to tell you that I feel something isn't right with your son and you may want to consider having Jimmy evaluated by a specialist.'

I started to feel my body temperature rise quickly, I suddenly wished I had taken off my coat before I sat down. I looked down at my hands, at the folders lying on the table, at anything but into Mrs. Wood's eyes. I felt like an armadillo waddling across a west Texas highway – caught in the headlights of an oncoming 18-wheeled truck. I froze and waited.

During the next minute or two that Mrs. Wood spoke, little she said registered in my consciousness. My head was still racing from the first salvo. 'How do you feel about what I've told you?' It was Mrs. Wood. My guess was she has had to break the bad news to other parents and could sense my shock.

'You do get right to the point,' I said, forcing a laugh that sounded a little too shaky. I struggled to maintain my composure. As I began to verbalize my thoughts to Mrs. Wood, I was surprised to hear myself telling her that while her observations caught me off guard and upset me, I had the same suspicions myself. What troubled me was that she seemed to be able to see a depth to Jimmy's problem that had somehow eluded me. Pangs of 'mother guilt' started to creep into my thoughts.

I knew Jimmy was having trouble socializing at school. After three years, he still hadn't made any friends. When I asked my son the names of some of the other children in his class, he couldn't tell me a single one. What was puzzling to the staff was that Jimmy wasn't seeking out other children in the traditional sense and didn't seem to care. Jimmy often seemed to be in his 'own little world' and would not pay attention or even participate in Circle Time.

In addition to the troubles with socialization, there were communication difficulties too. Many times the teachers had a hard time understanding Jimmy's way of talking. He often took dialog from videos that he watched at home and would endlessly use it when talking with the teachers and students in the class. One day, I picked him up from class and the teacher, Mrs. Wood, wanted to know what Jimmy meant when he said, 'You're Mama is a snowblower!' I asked her in what context the phrase was used. Mrs. Wood said that she was telling Jimmy to clean up the toys and get ready for Circle Time.

'He's mad at you for telling him to put the toys away,' I said to Mrs. Wood who looked even more puzzled. Then I had to explain that in the movie *Short Circuit*, the robot character Johnny-5 used that line of dialog in the movie when he was angry. All the while, it never occurred to me that my having to translate Jimmy's conversations for the teachers was anything but a quirky phase he was going through.

'Since starting school this Fall, Jimmy has been acting strangely in class,' Mrs. Wood continued. So there was more. The teacher could see I was getting lost in my thoughts and was trying to get my attention again.

Mrs. Wood described how Jimmy had recently become aggressive with the other students. Not only did this startle me, this was confusing to the staff at the school too. In their two year's experience with Jimmy, they found him to be a sweet, placid boy. Now Mrs. Wood was telling me of Jimmy's odd behavior towards other classmates and I was beginning to wonder if there was a Jekyll/Hyde thing going on. I am not one of those mothers who lives in a constant state of denial, believing that their child never does anything wrong, but the things she said my son was doing made it hard for me to believe that she was talking about *my* son.

Jimmy had been taught to share at home but, according to Mrs. Wood, he would become enraged if somebody was playing with 'his' toy. The problem was, they really weren't his toys, they belonged to the school. But in Jimmy's mind they were *his*. Mrs. Wood described how Jimmy would walk around the classroom during free play time, pick out an unsuspecting classmate and do something to purposely annoy him.

'It's like he wants to get their attention, but he doesn't know how,' said Mrs. Wood. A strange contradiction. Five minutes ago she was telling me Jimmy couldn't care less about making friends with the other classmates and now she is saying that he is trying to get their attention – either that, or he is trying to drive the other students away with offensive behavior. Now, I was confused too.

Class snack time was a struggle too. Mrs. Wood described how Jimmy would decide a certain chair was *his* and pity the poor clueless classmate who had the misfortune to sit in that particular seat. Jimmy would grab the offender by the scruff of the neck and yank him out of the chair with all the finesse of a bar bouncer.

'He isn't happy unless he gets to sit in the same seat everyday,' said Mrs. Wood.

By this time, I was starting to feel annoyed with my son. He had been taught good manners at home and I was feeling angry that he had felt he could act so rudely at school. I was embarrassed that Jimmy was acting this way. I planned on reading my son the riot act and made a mental note to have his father do the same when he arrived home from work. This kind of behavior is unacceptable and no child of mine will have a reputation for being a bully.

But there was even more. Apparently Mrs. Wood had saved the biggie for last. 'I want to tell you about an incident that happened last week, which makes me feel an evaluation is necessary,' she said. Now she really had my attention.

After snack time, the class is led in small groups to the bathrooms for potty-time. The previous week, the school had been having trouble with the plumbing in one of the toilets in the boys' room, so the staff had locked the stall and had taped a sign to the door that said, 'closed'.

'When Jimmy didn't come back, we sent the assistant in to get him and she found him still in the bathroom standing in front of the closed stall,' said Mrs. Wood. 'He was banging his head against the locked door saying over and over, "Let me in! Let me in! Let me in!"'

I was stunned. Could she possibly be talking about my son? There was no reason to disbelieve this teacher. All she was doing was trying to help. Suddenly, I had the urge to leave the school as fast as I could because I felt an overwhelming need to give my son a long hug. My heart ached to hold him, to find out what seemed to be bothering him, to find out what was wrong, to let him know that everything would be all right. I was confident I could find out a perfectly reasonable explanation for Jimmy's recent behavior. However serious the problem was, I was sure that I could fix it in a few weeks' time.

During that 20-minute conference, everything about my life had changed. Now it was obvious to someone else besides myself that there was something wrong with my son and I would have to take an active role in getting him help. I couldn't ignore the tiny voices of my gut feelings any longer. How could I deny that her observations have truth when I've harbored the same thoughts and suspicions for the last two years? She had forced me to go back to a place in my heart where I wasn't comfortable going. Had I been a psychic, I would have been able to see that from this point on, everything about my life would be altered. My visions of little league practices, cub scouts, birthday parties and neighborhood friends running through the house would never become a reality. As I sat like Goldilocks in that tiny chair, I had no idea that the winds of my life had just shifted and would now blow in a new direction. My life-long expectations of having a family that was 'just right' would be eroded away and a new version of normalcy would take its place.

As I left the school, I assured Mrs. Wood that I felt her words had some validity. I sensed that, in her experience, when she had given parents bad news such as this, they go into denial and yank their kids out of her school the very next week. As I left, I thanked Mrs. Wood for her frankness and honesty with me. I told her that I thought that it took a great deal of courage for her to tell me this kind of sad news and I wanted her to know that I truly respected her for doing so. I left with the feeling that this lady just did me a huge favor.

I arrived home to find the phone ringing. The call was from my mother-in-law, whose emotion-filled voice implored me to find my husband Jim at work and tell him to rush to his father's hospital bedside. Pop's condition was rapidly deteriorating and the doctors didn't feel as though there was much time left. I called my husband out of a meeting and told him the news of his father. I then called my friend Susan who had been watching Jimmy and his younger sister Caroline for me that morning. She agreed to keep the kids that afternoon. I met my husband at the hospital and kept a vigil during the last hours of my father-in-law's valiant struggle. The long, long, hug I needed to give my son would have to wait a few more hours. When Pop died early the next morning, the needs of the family would have to take precedence over my son's.

Any thoughts of fixing Jimmy's problem would have to wait several more days. The storm was starting to gather and I didn't even have the time to start looking for an umbrella.

2

Looking Back

When I think back to the time Jimmy was born, he has always been a solemn fellow. Since all nine pounds of him emerged from the womb, he has worn a serious expression. In my first conversation with my father after Jimmy was born, I remember telling him his grandson's face was so stern that if we stuck a bowler hat on him and gave him a cigar, he would look just like Winston Churchill.

It seemed like it took forever for Jimmy to give me a big, open smile. The first time I remember him smiling broadly at me was at Christmas time, when he was a little over four months old. I had put him in his infant seat on the dining room table where I was working with wrapping paper. As I talked and looked at him, I noticed his first gummy smile. I was so struck by this milestone, that I grabbed a camera and luckily got him to smile again for a picture.

After Jimmy was born, I was anxious to get him home from the hospital but found we had to contend with a few speed bumps first. Although he was described as healthy and had two Apgar scores of nine, the doctors told us that Jimmy was jaundiced and would have to come back to the hospital for a few Bilirubin treatments after his release. On top of that, the doctors also noticed a hip click. We were advised to triple-diaper him and take him in for an x-ray to see if any hip dysplasia had developed.

The first few days home really didn't feel restful. Jim and I ended up dragging ourselves across town for Bilirubin treatments, check-ups and the x-ray. Thankfully, Jim was able to clear his work schedule to help with this. Had I been on my own to make all these hospital trips, I would have been a nervous wreck.

My husband doted on his new son. He was as anxious as I to get him home from the hospital too. The first day was a wonderment. As Jim and I sat at the table for lunch, we were startled to hear Jimmy's cries coming from the nursery after his first at-home nap. We were both accustomed to such a quiet house. 'I guess we'll be getting used to a new "roommate",' smiled Jim, as he rushed up from his meal to greet his son. He took every opportunity to interact with Jimmy. Diapers were changed even if they didn't need changing. Jim gave Jimmy his first bath at home. How gentle he was! This was a wonderful part of my husband's personality that I had not had the pleasure of meeting up until now.

Jimmy slept well during the day but seemed to want to stay awake at night. He had his days and nights mixed up from the very beginning. My first indication of this was at four in the morning the day after I delivered him. I had instructed the nursery 'breast feed on demand' but as I sat up groggily in bed, I realized with a reluctant pleasure that I could recognize his lusty cries as the nursery staff wheeled him down the hall. This is what motherhood is all about? All I wanted was some sleep.

The same thing happened the second night. I sat up in bed in the middle of the night, hearing the unmistakable cries of my firstborn and the squeak of the wheels of the nursery cart being wheeled towards my room. Half-apologetically, the nurse placed Jimmy in my arms, muttering something about how much he cried in the nursery. I sensed with mild amusement that the nursery staff was only too happy to get rid of him and although I was tired, I was pleased to see my little guy for the nocturnal visit. I resigned myself to sleeping in the daytime until I could set up a schedule once I got home.

It seemed like all Jimmy wanted to do was eat. My milk came in right on schedule. Having been flat-chested all my life, being engorged with milk was suddenly the essence of womanhood. For the first time in my life, I actually had cleavage. Jimmy learned to suck from the breast right away. He would do 20 minutes on one side and 20 minutes on the other – every two hours.

My mother flew in to help me with the new baby. I was grateful for her help because I had no idea what I was doing. At that point, I was just operating on instinct and the few baby-care classes that were offered by the Ob-Gyn group. The first thing she noticed was Jimmy's screwed up sleeping schedule. A proponent of Dr. Benjamin Spock and Dr. Richard Ferber, who pioneered the 'let the baby cry' approach, Mom's first suggestion was to let Jimmy cry a little while during the night time hours to see if he would quickly settle back to sleep. Her suggestions about setting up a schedule made perfect sense to me. The ideas went along with everything I had heard and read. I was committed to the 'Ferberizing' strategy. At that point, I'd do anything to get some sleep.

Jimmy was a demanding customer. The first night we let him cry for two minutes, the next night, three minutes, then later in the week, seven minutes. Even though I would gently coo to him from the hall to let him know I was near, he was relentless. My mother was surprised at how strong-willed Jimmy was.

After several days we made little progress. Jim, by then back at work, couldn't stand the crying and groused at my mother's style of parenting. 'I'm telling you he's hungry and you need to get up and feed him,' he argued in hushed tones so my mother couldn't hear. As Jimmy's crying became more intense, the more agitated Jim became. During one early morning episode, when he had had enough, Jim walked out of our bedroom, past my mother who was standing watch in the hallway, got Jimmy out of his crib and delivered him to me for feeding. I was angry. I felt that he had undone several nights' worth of work. My mother was annoyed too. In Jim's view, we were not properly taking care of Jimmy. The friction between Jim and my mother wasn't exactly what I needed to start out this new chapter in my life.

When it came time for Jimmy's one-week check-up, Jim felt a sense of vindication. The pediatrician weighed Jimmy and noted a weight loss. He wrote 'failure to thrive' on Jimmy's medical chart. I was confused. 'But Doc,' I said. 'This baby is feeding every two hours around the clock and I'm barely getting any sleep.' I knew my breasts were not dry, I was leaking breast milk all over the place!

'It's your mother's half-baked idea to let him cry,' said Jim, clearly offended that his son would want for food and it was all the fault of his mother-in-law. The bemused pediatrician, who kept silent during our discussion, seemed puzzled that Jimmy was feeding so often yet still seemed hungry, as evidenced by the weight loss. He suggested a formula supplement, which I was only too happy to try. Anything to keep my baby healthy and my husband happy.

I was exhausted. We had a new baby who was having troubles adjusting to life outside the womb. I was killing myself staying up half the night (and most of the day) feeding him. The realities of post-partum depression were starting to hit. The good thing about it was that I finally had a beautiful baby (and a set of breasts that I'd only dreamed about).

Things improved the next week. Jimmy took to the bottle and started chugging down the formula. He gained weight quickly after that and started to sleep for longer periods during the night. Jim was visibly relieved. I felt nothing but guilt. I had been starving my baby. The hip-click issue was later resolved when the x-rays revealed no abnormality. Jimmy was given a clean bill of health.

Now that all the issues that had been weighing us down had been resolved, Jim and I felt a huge sense of closure. The hip was growing normally. At last, Jimmy was gaining weight and beginning to grow. We quickly settled into a routine. I would get up at night for the feedings, Jim always took the early morning feeding just before he left for work. Some days, I would lie in bed and smile sleepily as I listened to Jim talk to Jimmy during those early morning feedings. We were beginning what I thought would be a normal, uneventful life.

3

Now, What do We Do?

We didn't know it at the time, but the death of my father-in-law was a major point of transition in our lives. 'Pop' was only 59 years old when he passed away from cancer. He had quietly suffered the regimen of cat scans, surgeries and chemo treatments for five years. The first inkling of trouble that Jim and I ever had was one of those 'I've had a little surgery – nothing to worry about,' phone calls just after Jimmy was born.

Jimmy is named after his father, who is named after his father. When I was pregnant and the topic of names for our baby was discussed, there was no option other than naming a son after the father. In my husband's mind, I had no choice if our firstborn was a son. The practice of naming one's son after the father and grandfather is a common practice in Europe and America.

Jimmy always called his grandfather 'Pop'. My mother-in-law, whose eldest brother was also named Jim, often referred to her husband as 'Flingie' in endearing terms. I called my husband Jimmy until our son was born, after that, I just called him Jim. A few years after the death of his father, I began calling my husband 'Flingie' at about the same time that Jimmy announced that he wanted to be called just 'Jim' or 'son'. Pop called Jimmy 'Jiminy', taking the name from the little cricket character in the *Pinocchio* movie. Trying to keep all the 'Jims' straight to my side of the family resulted in some comical phone calls that were reminiscent of the old 'Whose on first?' comedy routine.

My husband was devastated at the death of his father. He was sure that Pop would win the latest battle with cancer. After all, Pop had gone to the hospital several times over the course of the disease and had always come home. There was no thought in his mind that this time it would be any different.

I felt at a loss to try and console my husband. Getting through the arrangements for the funeral was a very difficult thing for him. He openly wept. The children, especially Jimmy, just watched the whole scene unfold in our living room, their faces emotionless. The sight of their father crying was something they had never seen, nor had I for that matter. My husband had a bond with his father that I never really quite understood. On the surface, they did not seem very close, yet the attachment was there and the pain was horrible with the realization that his father was gone.

The morning Pop died, the family gathered in our living room, stunned. My husband was the first to arrive. His mother, who the children lovingly called 'Nanny', came shortly afterward. As the children stood in the hallway peering at the family all bawling our eyes out, Jimmy entered the room and asked, 'Where's Pop?'

With my heart in my throat, I took the children in my arms and explained, 'Pop died. He went to live with Heavenly Father.'

'Oh,' Jimmy said, his face devoid of any emotion. 'We sure are going to miss him.' And as the children sat on our laps, we all hugged them tightly and cried for the better part of an hour. Jimmy took the sad news very matter-of-factly. He showed no concern at all. If anything, he was a bit perplexed as to why this news of Pop's leaving would have us all in a dither. In his mind, Pop went to live in a very nice place, wasn't coming back, we would all miss him, and catch up to him at a later time when it was our turn to live in heaven. Caroline sat on her Nanny's lap and patted her wet cheeks from time to time.

As the years wear on and more and more of my son's personality emerges, the more I see that Jimmy and his grandfather are two peas in a pod. Pop and Jimmy were both quiet, gentle souls.

They both never liked a whole bunch of noise or commotion in the house. Jimmy often put his fingers in his ears at the slightest sound elevation. For some odd reason, sounds would bother Jimmy. Sometimes, gauging by the look on my son's face, these instances would be quite painful. We had his hearing checked several times and all the tests came back normal. It was not unusual to see my son walking around, or watching TV with his fingers stopping up his ears. Pop had a sensitivity to noise too and his way of coping would be to retreat to the back porch for a smoke to escape the din.

Both Jims are particular about their clothes. Fussy Flings are a family tradition. I remember grousing to Nanny, that my son was acting like a spoiled brat for refusing to wear anything but fleece pants, certain brands of athletic socks, and cotton shirts. She started to giggle across the kitchen table and said, 'We all know who that sounds like.' I figured if she put up with it for zillions of years, I guess I could too, and I had better stop whining about it. Flannel shirts and soft fleece pants were a staple of Pop's wardrobe. When he was a youngster, his mother had to take his dungarees and line them with flannel because he couldn't stand the rough fabric rubbing his legs. Pop always wore cotton socks. He hardly ever wore a suit. Then again, he rarely put himself in the situation where he had to wear one. My husband commented to me how he was pleased when his father wore a blue suit at our wedding. At the time, I was confused why this was such a *cause célèbre*, but in hindsight, I realize that donning a suit for our wedding was a life event for my father-in law. It was the only time I ever saw him wear one.

Every time I see my son in shorts, I see Pop's knobby knees. Both 'Jims' are creatures of habit. Pop used to park himself in his reclining easy-chair, remote control in one hand, a can of Sour Balls hard candy in the other. When I first joined the family, I received a friendly warning that I wasn't to sit in Pop's recliner or I would be met with a scowl. The only person who could get away with sitting in his easy-chair was Jimmy and later, his little sister. One scene that lasts in my mind is the picture of the two Jims sitting together in the easy chair, sucking on those nasty-tasting candies.

Pop's funeral was just as he would have liked it. Short, sweet, and to the point. There was no lengthy pontificating by the clergy. Pop wanted, and got, a simple graveside ceremony. He wanted no crowds of mourners in a church vestry. Just a few close friends. Afterward, Nanny requested that the kids be brought to the family home for the open house. I sensed that she, as did I, wanted to have the children around. In her case, she wanted their cloud-free, innocent faces. For me, it was more a matter of distraction. I knew that once the funeral was over and all the people had finished paying their respects, I was going to have a crisis on my hands.

As luck would have it, one of Jim's cousins was a teacher of special education. On the back porch of the family home during the post-funeral get together, Jim and I discussed the situation with Jimmy and the preschool teacher's observations. One of the issues that we were wrestling with was whether or not to seek help from the school officials, since Jimmy would be attending public school that next year, or take care of things on our own. We didn't want our son to be labeled 'special'. To us, the term 'special' had negative connotations. Her advice to us proved to be among the most valuable that we received.

'Get help now, while he is very young,' she said. 'Believe me, it is better to have the label now than for Jimmy to experience failure in a regular classroom. I have worked with so many students who have been placed in regular classes, who have failed year after year. They end up accumulating all the extra emotional baggage of frustration – in addition to the disability itself – and I'll tell you that it is tougher for these kids to deal with the low self esteem than the disability itself.'

As Jim and I felt the desiccated leaves swirl around the back patio, we let her words sink in. A clear image popped into my mind of what a future would be like if we did nothing to help our son. We would have a boy who would be angry, frustrated and suicidal. I gave an involuntary shudder. There was no way I wanted that to happen to my son. I resolved to look for help from outside sources. A small voice in my subconscious urged me to seek help, a voice that I would learn to rely on heavily to get me successfully through life's disasters – both big and small. I glanced at my husband and sensed that he had experienced the same epiphany. The sooner we got help for Jimmy, the better off he would be. We knew there was no other way.

After the visit with Mrs. Wood, and armed with the advice of Jim's cousin, we scheduled an appointment with our pediatrician. My husband and I had no idea that this consultation was the first step on to a five-year medical merry-go-round. As we nervously sat in the doctor's office, we both felt some embarrassment and shame at having to tell the pediatrician that our son was ill-behaved at school. I had every confidence that just a few weeks of intensive behavior modification therapy would be all we'd need to whip my son right into shape. By the time he would enter public school, his developmental 'speed bump' would be long behind us.

Our conference with the doctor lasted about 20 minutes. I quickly rattled off as much of the observed behaviors as I could. He jotted down, 'possible ADD? Perceptually Impaired? Psychological?' in Jimmy's file.

By this time, we had been associated with the pediatric practice for four years. Our doctor knew the children fairly well and was even in the delivery room when Caroline was born by Cesarean section. During the course of those four years, we had seen him for more than our share of stitches for Jimmy. Just before we moved from California, Jimmy tripped and gashed his head against the corner of a wall, which required three stitches in the hospital emergency room. After we moved, Jimmy again tripped in my mother-in-law's kitchen (with four adults helplessly standing by watching) and split his lip open – three more stitches. A month later, he was jumping off my bed and did another number under his chin.

Chalk up another five stitches. Around this time, we started calling him 'Mr. Klutz'.

'It sounds like you are looking for Jimmy to get involved in some social skills therapy,' said the pediatrician, 'We happen to have an excellent person who does this on a part-time basis right here in the office.' He scribbled her name on a piece of paper and handed it to me. I could make out the first name – Deanie. But the doctor's typical physician-style penmanship had all but butchered the last name. I was too shy to ask him to decipher his handwriting for me.

When my husband and I prepared to leave, we stopped at the front desk where I scheduled an appointment with Deanie Yasner, the social skills therapist. A few days before our first appointment, I received a phone call. On the other end of the line was a delicate voice with a heavy southern drawl. It was Deanie. For the first few minutes of our conversation, her southern accent distracted me. Hearing her voice eerily reminded me of my own grandmother, who was raised in Western Tennessee. As it turned out, Deanie hailed from the Volunteer State as well. I immediately liked her. I briefly went over the concerns that had come up in the conference with Mrs. Wood and we agreed to eight sessions (one per week, 30 minutes each) after which, we would see where we stood and re-assess where to go from there.

'Are your services covered by medical insurance?' I asked, fearing the worst.

Unfortunately, although she was an expert in social development, Deanie only had a Master's Degree. To get on board with the insurance companies as a provider of social skills services, you need a minimum of a Ph.D. she explained. Her fee was $25 per session and yes, she would take a personal check.

I hung up anticipating the song and dance routine I would have to do to convince my husband that shelling out $200 for social skills was worth the money that we just didn't have. I broke the news to him at dinner. His response was just as I anticipated. He was thoroughly annoyed.

'What do you mean this is not covered by insurance?!' he hissed. 'You are going to the doctor's office for the service. Why can't they bill it out of their accounting office?'

'Because the bottom line is that she doesn't qualify as a provider under any medical policy that is available to us – probably to anyone.' I countered. Never before had we been faced with a situation that was not covered by our medical insurance. We both just stared at each other and didn't quite know what to say.

'Does Jimmy really need this?' he queried, his eyes squinting. I could see that his visions of 'therapy' were tantamount to the touchy-feely Lamaze classes that we took together before Jimmy was born. The word therapy is not in his vocabulary. The thought of his son – his namesake – having to undergo therapy so he can have friends and act properly in class!!?? It was all a bit too much for him to digest.

'Who is this Deanie person anyway?' he asked. 'How do we know we are doing the right thing?'

'She comes highly recommended by the doctor and my gut tells me that she and Jimmy would be a good match.' I said, hoping that he wouldn't ask me to give the reasons why I thought it would work. 'She reminds me of my grandmother' just wasn't going to cut it as a good solid reason for a decision to spend $200.

The day of the first appointment with Deanie came. I dressed Jimmy and his sister Caroline, packed them into the car and made our way to the doctor's office.

'Where are we going?' asked Jimmy.

'We are going to visit a lady named Deanie,' I said, wondering how I was going to explain this to my son in a way that was palatable. 'We're going to see her at the doctor's office.'

'Is she a doctor?' he asked. Lately, Jimmy had been reluctant to go to the doctor's office. I couldn't really put my finger on just why. Other than the stitches, which we took care of in the emergency room, there was no emotional trauma associated with our going there. Jimmy had always complied with his immunizations like a good soldier. The only thing I noticed was that he put his fingers in his ears when we came into the waiting room. This behavior was becoming very common in many situations. Despite having his hearing tested, the doctors kept telling us not to worry, his hearing was normal.

'No, she is not a doctor,' I said. 'She is like a teacher. The doctor lets her have one of his rooms at the office to use like a classroom.'

'But I already have a school,' Jimmy said. I glanced in the rearview mirror to see what his reaction was. I saw the trademark scowl that reminded me so much of his grandfather. I could easily sense that he was not very happy having to go sit around at the doctor's office.

Once we arrived in the waiting area, Caroline immediately started to play cooperatively with the other children. Jimmy walked over to a rocking horse and attempted to tell the child who was riding that the rocking horse was his toy and that the other child had to get off.

My face became warm. The other boy's mother was looking at me like I was a large beetle. Not that I blame her for being annoyed, but I wanted to scream, 'This anti-social behavior is why I'm here!'

'Jimmy,' I said in my 'don't mess with me' voice, loud enough for all the moms in the waiting room to hear. 'It's not your horse. It's the doctor's horse. You will have a turn in five minutes.'

Jimmy just gave me a blank look and proceeded to grab the shirt of the kid who was sitting on the horse. It was like I hadn't even uttered the words. I was the invisible mom. The kid on the horse started to protest loudly. Jimmy gritted his teeth and dug in his heels on the issue. In his mind, this was *his* horse. The other boy *had* to get off his horse. He *always* played on this horse when he came to the doctor's office. The other kid's mom was giving me dagger looks as I walked over to physically restrain Jimmy.

'Jimmy?' came a voice from across the room. A new voice. A voice with a southern accent.

Jimmy stopped. I paused. Everyone in the waiting area turned to look. I was saved by the southern belle. There in the doorway was Deanie.

Jimmy looked up at me. 'It's time to go in now,' I said taking his hand off the other kid's shirt. We walked over to where she was waiting. Deanie was what songwriter Randy Newman describes as a 'short person'. Just an 'itty-bitty thang' as they would say back in Tennessee. She was so small that she would be lucky to find a big enough size on the petite rack. I was dumbstruck. She was a younger version of my grandmother.

Maybe it was her size that drew Jimmy to her immediately. Perhaps it was the voice too. There was nothing threatening about Deanie from a kid's perspective. She wore a denim skirt and comfortable-looking sweater and was not so much taller than my son. Although Jimmy barely knew his great-grandmother, perhaps there was a subconscious feeling of safety with Deanie. Her voice personified the iron hand/velvet glove analogy that one hears so often associated with women of the American south. It had a pleasant lilting quality to it, yet as evidenced by everyone's reaction in the waiting area, Deanie's voice could command the attention of everyone in the room.

When it came time for Jimmy to separate from me and go to one of the patient rooms, he seemed willing to go with Deanie, yet he seemed anxious. His fingers went in his ears.

'What's the matter Jimmy?' Deanie asked. 'Why do you have you fingers in your ears?'

'There's a baby crying,' Jimmy said. 'Tell the doctor to make the baby stop crying.'

'I guess he can't stand the thought of a baby crying,' I said. Oddly, the only baby I could hear crying was in another part of the building. 'He must have a very tender heart to be so worried about a baby.'

'Jimmy. Come with me,' said Deanie, extending her hand. 'We'll go talk to the doctor and see what we can do to help that baby.' And with his left finger poked in one ear and his right ear pressed against his right shoulder, Jimmy and Deanie disappeared hand-in-hand into the maze of patient rooms. Our journey had begun.

4

Back to Basics

It was one of those days when I became obsessed with the thought of throwing the inventor of the VCR into a river full of leeches.

Caroline and Jimmy were sitting at the kitchen table while I was assembling peanut butter and jelly sandwiches. Jimmy was clearly annoyed with his sister. As I glanced over, I was clueless as to why. Yet, his temper was at a slow boil and unless I intervened, the top would pop off Jimmy's 'pressure cooker'.

As I placed the sandwiches in front of the kids, Jimmy announced, 'This little fart of a robot is giving me the red-ass.'

Not again! Another snippet from his favorite movie. Only this time, the language was not acceptable. In the movie, *Short Circuit,* the character Scroter uses the same line to express his anger at the robot who escapes from the research facility. Now my son has swiped the dialog to express his annoyance at his sister.

'Listen to me Mister,' I said firmly. 'I don't like to hear "red-ass" talk in my house. That's video-talk.'

Jimmy scowled as I continued, shaking my finger at him. 'Does Daddy say "red-ass?" Does Mommy say "red-ass?"' I waited for Jimmy to answer. After a long time, he shook his head 'No.'

'Then you don't say "red-ass" any more – got it? Now eat your sandwich!'

I looked at Caroline, who had finished about half of her sandwich during my lecture. She gave a smarmy smile and started tapping her foot on the table leg nearest her brother. It was just a little thing, yet he was going bonkers over it – literal melt-down. I couldn't understand why Jimmy was having a problem with his sister tapping her foot, and wished that he would cut her some slack.

I blew.

'Jimmy! Eat your sandwich! Caroline! Knock it off!'

We (or I) enjoyed a moment of silence.

'Don't want this sandwich,' Jimmy said. 'Need another one.'

'There's nothing wrong with your sandwich,' I growled. 'Eat your sandwich!'

'Can't eat this sandwich. It's square. I *need* a triangle sandwich.'

Normally when I make a sandwich, I cut the bread crosswise fashion so the pieces of the sandwiches were triangle-shaped. This time, I was so distracted playing referee to my children that I cut the bread in half, and half again, making four small squares. If my son thought I would dump his sandwich in the trash simply because it wasn't in little triangular pieces, he was living in the wrong house!

'I'm NOT making you another sandwich,' I bellowed. 'You will have to eat the one you have.'

'But I can't.'

'Yes you can. Quit acting like a spoiled brat.'

'But I *can't* !

'OK. Then you will be a hungry boy.'

The sandwich went uneaten. Jimmy's hunger didn't overcome his stubbornness. His willfullness amazed me at times. Most kids will back down when they are met with parental authority. Not Jimmy. With my son you needed the negotiation skills of a United Nations diplomat to strike a deal and make the peace.

I poured milk into the kids' glasses and urged them to hurry up and finish their meal, even though it was clear that Jimmy's sandwich would never touch his lips.

'Ahh,' said Jimmy, raising his glass. 'Just the way I like it. Shaken, but not stirred.'

That darn movie again! Jimmy had seen *Short Circuit* on cable TV several months ago and had managed to pop a blank videocassette into our VCR and tape the whole movie. He had watched it over and over and was absolutely obsessed with the little robot in the movie. He would run around the house telling me he was 'Johnny-5' and needed 'Input – more input!' Every conversation that anyone would have with my son always somehow managed to steer to on the subject of robots, particularly 'Johnny-5.' He knew all the lines of dialog and would use them to communicate. He was generally pretty much on-topic, only in this case he was talking about his glass of milk, rather than the gin and tonic that the character was quaffing in the movie. Most people would expect that Jimmy was borrowing this line from one of the James Bond movies. But Jimmy was into robots, not 007. The problem was that the dialog meant nothing if you hadn't seen the movie, but to us, he made perfect sense.

'C'mon!' I urged the kids. 'We have to hurry and get in the car or we'll be late for our appointment with Deanie.' I learned early on that if I was going to get my son to do anything, it would require plenty of up front warning. In this case, the appointment wasn't for another 45 minutes. Although it was a short drive, I still had to change the kids into clean clothes and get into the car. Barnum and Bailey's logistics were a piece of cake compared to the pre-planning I had to do for a simple ride to the store.

'Let's move it kids – STAT!' Jimmy looked at me, a bit startled. He immediately got out of his chair and went towards the bedroom. Now I was talking his movie-dialog language. If Jimmy could pretend, so could I.

In the bedrooms, Jimmy and Caroline proceeded to undress themselves, although Caroline always seemed to be quicker than Jimmy. Always the slowpoke, Jimmy generally ended up sitting on his bed staring off into space. After ping-ponging between the kids' bedrooms, as usual I ended up spending most of my time getting

Jimmy moving. Fortunately, Caroline was a pretty independent child.

'Jimmy to earth!' I said, trying to draw his attention back to changing his clothes. I put his pants and shirt next to him on the bed. He just stared at them.

'Jimmy! Put your clothes on!' I shrieked, in an attempt to rouse him from the far-away place that consumed him. Why did I have to do *everything* for this child? He was a five-year-old and should be able to dress himself. After all, his younger sister could do just fine. I assumed that Jimmy's lack of motivation was his way of getting back at me over the sandwich incident. I felt manipulated and didn't appreciate it one bit. Jimmy picked up the pants and fiddled with them like a fussy eater pushing food from side to side on a dinner plate. First he weakly attempted one leg, then the other.

Enough! I grabbed the pants from his hands and roughly put them on. Then I grabbed his shirt and flung it over his head. Jimmy put his arms through. 'See!' I said through clenched teeth, 'You really COULD put your clothes on if you tried harder.' Then I wiggled his socks over his feet and put his sneakers on. I was fighting tears as I tied the laces.

By the time we found our coats and were ready to get in the car, I was in a fine lather. As I adjusted the mirrors on the car and backed down the driveway, I quietly wondered to myself whether I was cut out for the job of mothering. Surely all my friends who have kids are living the same hectic life than I am. They seemed to be handling things just peachy. What was I doing wrong? Sure, they complained of exhaustion at the end of the day, but they didn't seem as angry or frustrated. But here it was, barely noon, and I had reached my breaking point. What's wrong with me? Why can't I be a better mother?

'Our young man is a little bit grouchy today,' I said breezily to Deanie upon arriving for our appointment. Actually, I was the one who was the grouch. Although I was wiped out emotionally, I was putting on my 'best face'. Maybe I was nuts, but I was actually looking forward to a half-hour of solace hanging around in a pediatrician's waiting room with a bunch of sick children. I could read the business section of the newspaper while Caroline became infected with all manner of diseases. If it meant a short break from Jimmy, I considered it a fair trade. At the very least, I could hold off on my thoughts of a vacation getaway to a Turkish prison.

After the session, Deanie emerged with Jimmy who made a beeline for the rocking horse. Thankfully it was not in use. We sat down in a secluded corner of the waiting room and she opened her file. Out of the corner of my eye, I tried to scan her notes. There were so many observations and comments listed that I hardly could process what I was trying to surreptitiously read.

'Who is Johnny Five?' she began. For what must have been the 100th time that month, I explained Jimmy's obsession with the movie. 'He must watch it twice a day,' I said. 'It's like he's driven to it. If he doesn't get his daily dose, he is unbearable. Jim and I taught him how to use the VCR and remote control, and now we're sorry we did. He presses the re-wind button and plays the same segments over and over again. I'm so sick of some of those lines that I want to scream.' Deanie didn't say anything. She was observing Jimmy at play in the waiting room. I knew she was carefully considering my words. Surely she was thinking that I was a weak excuse of a mother to let her son stay glued in front of the TV all day long.

'Well, let me tell you what I think about Jimmy so far,' she said. I got out my notebook. Luckily, as a journalist, I took notes for a living. My husband was going to want a report on the session and I had to write everything down or I would forget it. My notes would later prove to be an *ad hoc* 'Deanie-Diary' that would help me see how much progress Jimmy had made. During these de-briefing sessions, Deanie wasn't only helping Jimmy, she was teaching me as well.

Deanie told me that Jimmy had a hard time communicating because he didn't have a grasp of the basics of language. Even though he could speak, Jimmy wasn't able to start or maintain a conversation. The way Deanie explained it, the real reason he was resorting to bullying behavior in school was because he wasn't able to communicate his thoughts to the other children, nor could he recognize and understand the perspective of others. Deanie also seemed to think that Jimmy had difficulty correctly reading the facial expressions of the other children in his class. I was baffled! How could a child not intuitively pick up this skill? Everyone knows what a smile means! It's universal!

'Jimmy needs help with his abstract thinking,' said Deanie. I gave her a blank look. I could see that this was my first lesson in the language of disabilities. 'You will need to label his world,' she said. 'The kitchen is a great place to start. Ask him to go into the refrigerator and find all the fruit.' Deanie broadened her lesson to include hot things, cold things, hard and soft things. 'Use every minute of the day as a teaching opportunity,' she said. 'From now on, your role as his mother will be a coach and teacher.' I would label everything – emotions, behaviors, objects. It was like we had to assume Jimmy had just arrived from the depths of the Amazon jungle.

I was stunned. We were talking about directly teaching Jimmy things that I assumed he already knew. My mind started to wander. I was reminded of the scene in the movie *The Miracle Worker*, where Annie Sullivan is racing around the room with Helen Keller naming every object in sight. She's telling me that we have to start all over again with Jimmy.

'This is going to be a new thing for you,' she continued. 'You will have to be completely non-judgmental when you teach Jimmy and leave emotion out of it.' I cringed at the thought of the bedroom episode earlier that afternoon. I had clearly let my emotions get the better of me.

'Jimmy has weak processing skills,' Deanie said. 'This affects his perceptions in many areas, such as body image and non-verbal communication.' Most of us have an innate sense of how our bodies are supposed to relate in a group setting. When we're in an elevator, we all instinctively stand facing the door. Or we all have a good sense of when we're getting too close to someone else, thus violating the unspoken personal space rule. For kids like Jimmy, all these silent 'rules' do not come naturally. They have to be directly taught. Deanie suggested that I buy the game 'Twister' and play it with Jimmy. 'Don't use the spinner,' she advised. 'Just start out with simple commands like, 'put your right hand on the blue dot.'

'Deanie also explained how Jimmy was unable to recognize the feelings and emotions of others. This was stunning to me. He couldn't correctly read another child's smile as an invitation to play. It was now my full-time job to use real-life examples as a teaching tool to help Jimmy understand facial expressions.

'The most important thing you need to work on first is providing structure for Jimmy – set up a schedule,' she said. Earlier, we had discussed Jimmy's jack-rabbit eating habits, which were annoying everyone in the family. 'You're going to start making rules for everything,' smiled Deanie. 'The first being that children must ask permission before leaving the dinner table.' She instructed me to re-enforce this rule every time we sat down to a meal, with the hope that this will curb Jimmy's desire to eat-n-run, then return. 'Be a drill sergeant about this in the beginning and as the kids get used to the idea, you can relax a bit,' she said. 'It's easier to let off later rather than escalate enforcement of a rule.' Structure was a huge need that my son had. Unfortunately, it was my weakest area. We also discussed the issue of Jimmy dressing himself. 'Never do for a child what he can do for himself,' Deanie stressed. 'Lay out his clothes for him in the morning and at night. Be very matter of fact about it, stand over him if need be, encourage him, but you are not doing it for him any more. If you are late, you are late.'

Deanie and I also discussed personal accountability. 'Jimmy needs to be responsible for his toys and cleaning his room,' said Deanie. As with the clothes, I was no longer in the business of picking up toys. Jimmy was to do it himself now. 'You need to accept his level of mastery and not re-do his work,' Deanie cautioned. 'And Caroline can't do the work for him either.'

After about 20 minutes of discussion, Deanie closed her file and we set up our time for the next week. She suggested that I get hold of a copy of the book, *Children: The Challenge*, by Rudolf Dreikers and read it before next week's session. The road home led through a farm area of harvested cornfields. The spent stalks stretched on for miles creating a hypnotic effect. I thought of my son and his obsession with the little robot Johnny-5. The irony of it! Jimmy is like the little robot. Both need to learn the basic things in humanity. Jimmy had spent the last part of the month racing around the house muttering, 'Need input, need, input...' My heart ached. He was reaching out, asking for help, using the same language as the robot in the movie, and I hadn't heard him.

'Newton Crosby, P-H-Dork,' chanted Jimmy from the rear seat. I smiled. More video talk. How could I be annoyed with him? The only way my sweet son could communicate was to borrow lines from the videos he's watched. It was my job to give him the means to take his place with the rest of the children in his class. Mapping out my strategy would have to wait until tomorrow morning. Right now, I had to take the time to ponder the gargantuan task that lay ahead of me.

5

Kitchen Classroom

In every home, the kitchen table is the center of the universe, and our house is no exception. If the table could talk, think of the stories it could tell. There would be Jimmy's first birthday cake, and the time that I told my husband I was pregnant with Caroline. The kitchen table is the place where all is right with the world. In Jimmy's case, the kitchen table was probably the safest place in the world next to his bed. It seemed the right place to start teaching him the nuances of language and emotion.

We had been working with Deanie for a few weeks now, who said that Jimmy seemed to have no grasp of how to read the facial expressions of others, nor could he verbalize his feelings. Both Deanie and Mrs. Wood had remarked 'You never knew what he was thinking or feeling.'

Jimmy and I had devised the 'face-game'. It would be the first social-cognition therapy session in my 'kitchen classroom'. The first time we played the game, I began by asking him to mimic the expression on my face. For several minutes we matched facial contortions. I always started with a huge smile. Then I ran through the expressions of sad, angry, surprised, scared, and shy. All my expressions were wildly exaggerated so that Jimmy could discern the differences.

Then it would be Jimmy's turn. He would go through all the facial expressions that he could muster and I would mimic him. In the beginning, he could only show me a happy and sad face. As the weeks progressed, he was able to show me more subtle expressions like shyness. He got to enjoy the game so much that we only had to make eye contact to start the game. When he was finished with the silent game, he would put his head down on the table in exhaustion.

Later, as his abilities increased, I decided to add a verbal component to the game. I would ask Jimmy to make me a 'happy face'. I would go through all the expressions that we had practiced in the face-game, but this time I was requesting the faces on demand. I could tell that I was getting through to him when I could see a little smirk cross his lips. He was having fun. I would mimic along with him and the requests would get faster and faster until Jimmy would put his head down on the table, his signal that he'd had enough.

All this game-playing was laying the groundwork. Jimmy was learning to recognize a smile and match the word with the expression. For me, the greatest difficulty was explaining the emotion that matched the expression. Through mimicry, Jimmy was learning what a smile felt like on his own face. Often, we would resume the game in front of the bathroom mirror. I wanted him to see what the smiles looked and felt like on his own face. Jimmy's smiles looked like one of those cheesy, toothy grins that one might use when the in-laws show up unexpectedly for dinner. A nice start for a little boy who rarely smiled just three weeks ago.

I called my friend Susan to borrow a copy of the Dreikers book. Her parenting library was stocked to the gills with books on dealing with the unmanageable child. I plowed through most of the book in one evening. The author's common-sense approach appealed to me. I particularly like his ideas on providing consistency and having children experience the natural consequences of their decisions. He advocates having a house of rules and order. I wanted to use some of the techniques outlined in the book. The hardest part would be providing consistency.

During my next meeting with Deanie, I discussed what I had read and we came up with strategies to whip the house into shape.

Mealtimes had always been horrific. The kids were not getting any kind of consistency for mealtimes. Often it would depend on a phone call from my husband saying, 'Honey, I'm on my way,' which would send me scurrying to the stove. 'What you need to do is have dinner at the same time every night,' Deanie suggested, 'whether their father is there or not. Let the kids have dessert with their Daddy after he gets home.'

'But what do I do about the food?' Many times I would put the food on the table only to hear Jimmy announce, 'I'm not eating.'

'Just ignore him,' she said. 'When you put the food down in front of him, you tell him, "this is what we're having."'

'You also need to set-up food rules,' said Deanie. 'Jimmy needs to get permission first before taking any food or snacks out of the kitchen. This will give you more control of what he eats and when.' Deanie also stressed that the children need to ask for permission to leave the dinner table. 'Verbally go over this rule every time you sit down to eat,' she said. Up until now, Jimmy had been an 'eat-n-run' dinner companion. He would often eat and get up from the table, mill about the room and then sit back down and eat more.

'Be a fanatic about this in the beginning,' Deanie counseled.

The next night, I made one dinner. I tried the Deanie approach and got the usual 'I'm not eating' from Jimmy. I ignored it.

'This is what we're eating,' I said to both kids as matter-of-factly as I could muster. I had to stand tough or we would be eating 'Hamburger Helper' and macaroni and cheese the rest of our lives.

Jimmy ended up eating most of the food on his plate. Caroline held the line. She wouldn't even try the food. She nibbled on a few canned peaches, pushed her food from one side of the plate to the other and got down from the table hungry. I was surprised. If I had bet the odds in Las Vegas, I would have predicted Jimmy to be the willful one when it came to food.

There were other difficulties to deal with. We didn't know it at the time, but Jimmy's relationship with his father was slowly beginning to shift. Only did we realize years later that Jimmy was subconsciously pushing his father out of his life. The reason why, we did not know.

'It's as though Jimmy doesn't like me,' Jim said to me one night. 'Intellectually, I know that he loves me, but you've seen how he hardly even bothers to say "Hello" when I come home from work. He never comes running into my arms like Girly does. It's as though I am just in the way… just the guy who stops by to sleep here at night.'

He was right. While I had seen the way Jimmy was with his father, I never put the thought into what kind of impact it would have on Jim. I had always accepted my son's unresponsiveness as just a part of his personality. I was home all the time. Jimmy felt comfortable with me. He would touch me, or sit on my lap on occasion. I was satisfied with the little physical affection that I received from him, figuring that it was just Jimmy's way. I got more than enough cuddles from Caroline to fill the void. But to hear Jim's frustration shed a new light on things. He was right, Jimmy virtually ignored him and I hadn't really noticed the pain it must have been causing my husband. How could I be so self-absorbed in my own world (and that of my children) that I had failed to see things from my husband's point of view. I hurt for him.

At school, Jimmy was showing a little improvement. Mrs. Wood reported that he had played with another child and the aggression was rarely being seen. I was relieved. Deanie's work with him was taking root. The aggressive behavior was something that I was very worried about. Yet all she did was teach him the 'rules' of proper social conduct and a simple anger management technique: 'When something happens that makes you angry or you don't like, you say, "PHOOEY!"' Deanie explained to Jimmy that all kids get angry and that it was OK to have these feelings and you just say, 'Phooey'.

It was amazing how quickly Jimmy responded to concepts when they were presented to him as hard and fast 'rules'. When it was explained that children do not hit other children – period –

under any circumstances, Jimmy immediately stopped his bullying. For him, it was against the rules. Now this is not to say that he didn't smolder from afar when another child sat in 'his' special chair at snack time. But I was relieved that the physical aspect of the behavior was curbed.

Every day, before I dropped him off at school, I would go through the drill. 'Jimmy, what are the rules at school?' Through the car's rear-view mirror, I'd look at Jimmy in the rear seat. No response. It was as though I didn't exist.

'Jimmy!' I prompted. 'What are the rules at school?'

'No hitting the other kids. Sit during Circle Time. Use our inside voices. No running up the sliding board.'

'Right,' I said. 'And what do you say if someone makes you angry?'

'I say, PHOOEY!' Jimmy said, hitting his fist into the palm of his hand for emphasis.

'Good,' I coaxed. 'And then you tell Mrs. Wood why you are angry.'

Now that the aggression seemed to be gone, I was sure that we would just as quickly fix the other problems that seemed to be bothering Jimmy. But on my next visit with Deanie, I got an indication that making things right was not going to be as easy as solving the aggression problem.

Jimmy seemed happy and content to see Deanie this week for our session. They had spent the time on expressive language. Deanie taught Jimmy how to ask for a snack. When the session was over, Jimmy wanted to stay in the 'play-room' while Deanie came out to consult with me in the waiting area.

We talked about the progress we'd made and Deanie asked how my husband was dealing with all of this.

'I'm thinking that while he understands what you've been telling us about Jimmy, a little part of him still doesn't want to believe that there is a problem,' I said, retelling Jim's recent frustration with his son's unresponsiveness. 'It's like I have to push him hard to get him to pay attention to what I'm saying.'

Deanie said that she understood my frustration. Apparently I wasn't the first mother she'd worked with who had expressed the same feelings about the father. In her experience, the fathers were typically the last ones to come around and accept the idea that their child, especially their son, wasn't perfect in every way.

'So what you're saying is that I just need to be patient with Jim too,' I laughed. Deanie nodded.

'Jimmy is the most complex boy that I've ever worked with,' she said. 'There's something about him that I just can't put my finger on.' My maternal antennae shot up. I immediately thought of a thorny artichoke. Yes! Jimmy was as complex as an artichoke! Deanie and I are going to have to peel back a lot of thorny layers before we get to the heart of what's truly the issue with him.

'I think that we really ought to have Jimmy tested by a psychologist,' Deanie said. 'They have tests that can really show me where his areas of weakness are and can help me concentrate on the areas where he needs help.'

My hope of having all the wrinkles ironed out before Jimmy started public school in the fall was fading. I started to feel warm. My face began to perspire.

'Echo, Jimmy is probably not going to make it in a conventional Kindergarten class. Do you understand that?' said Deanie. I nodded. She knew just about everything else, so I might as well admit my deep-rooted fear that he'd be totally be lost, and fall through the cracks.

' I know – you're right,' I sadly said to Deanie. 'I just can't see him in a room with 25 other kids and being able to function. Just the noise level in the room will send him back into his own little world. The other kids won't be able to understand Jimmy. He'll have his fingers in his ears 90 percent of the time. The teacher will be so busy dealing with such a large class that he'll turn invisible. He won't be able to learn anything!'

'You might have to consider placing him in a special education classroom or going with a private school,' she said. 'At any rate, you will have to know exactly what you're dealing with. Jimmy needs educational testing. Psychologists are the ones who administer these kinds of tests. When you get the results, you will be able to make a good decision based on the best information possible.'

We discussed several strategies. Deanie recommended a psychologist she had a good relationship with who has a clinical practice in Princeton. Dollar signs flashed in front of my eyes.

After talking with Jim and finding out that our insurance did cover 80 percent of the psychologist's fees, I called and scheduled an appointment with Dr. Matthews for early in February. Later that week, I received in the mail an extensive set of questionnaires, one for me to fill out, and the other for Jimmy's teacher. The form consisted of pages and pages of questions about every aspect of Jimmy's life and early development. It took me a day to go through the paperwork. I was asked in minute detail about my pregnancy, Jimmy's first steps, when he babbled, when his first word was spoken, his eating habits, sleeping habits, bowel habits, if he picked his nose, was he a fussy eater, or overeater, was he stubborn, moody, disobedient, did he pay attention, was he physical with others – you name it!

The testing process with the psychologist went over three days. She wanted two sessions with Jimmy. The third session with the parents would be a presentation of her test results. I was very nervous. Jimmy could be so irrelevant at times. What if he said something bizarre and the psychologist thought he was crazy – or worse, thinks I am a bad parent?

The doctor's office was in an office building on the main drag in Princeton, New Jersey – a 20-minute ride from our home. 'Are we going to the witch's castle?' Jimmy asked as we pulled into a parking garage. Princeton University's landmark Firestone Hall looks like the castle of the Wicked Witch of the West in the movie

The Wizard of Oz. It was situated across the street from the doctor's office.

'No, not this time,' I said. 'We're going to visit a friend of Deanie's. She is a doctor.'

Jimmy scowled.

'Her name is Doctor Wendy,' I said cheerfully, 'just like in *Peter Pan.* She is a teacher-doctor, just like Deanie.'

'Will I get a shot?' asked Jimmy.

'No, silly,' I said softly. 'Dr. Wendy has no needles, no stethoscopes, not even a nurse. She's a teacher-doctor.'

We reached the office, and Dr. Matthews emerged from her inner sanctum. We visited briefly and I introduced Jimmy to her as 'Deanie's friend, Dr. Wendy.'

'Will I get a shot?' Jimmy asked skeptically. The doctor assured him that he would not. Jimmy then took her hand and went inside the office without a single protest. As the door closed, I felt as though I was handing the mind of my first-born over to a stranger. This was the first time I had ever felt like I had no control over a situation in my child's life.

Jimmy went through the two days of testing without incident and now it was time for Jim and I to get the report. We were both nervous. I had begun experiencing bouts of colitis and today was no exception. About halfway through the report, I had to excuse myself and quickly find the ladies room. I was very embarrassed about having to remove myself. But the doctor was very kind, and easy-going about the break. I was starting to warm up to her.

The doctor presented us with a nine-page psychological report. Neither my husband or I had ever seen one before and were amazed with the thoroughness. The tests that Jimmy had taken were IQ tests. To our relief, he had an average IQ. The doctor then went on about the different subtests, which I barely paid any attention to. I only heard that Jimmy's IQ was high enough to be considered an intelligent child. I tuned out terms like verbal and performance scales. It was all Greek to me. My eyes glazed over. I was on stress overload.

The final paragraph of her report was the stunning blow. This was the first time that my husband or I had heard the term, 'learning disabilities'. The doctor went on to talk about Jimmy's perceptual problems with social interactions. We had noticed that Jimmy didn't seem to recognize the meaning in the tone of voice that we used. For example, he never caught on to jokes we would tell him, or when I was angry, he seemed ambivalent. It was as though I was the invisible yelling mother. Dr. Matthews recommended the involvement of the special education people 'to insure Jimmy receive the services he needs at school.' I skipped over the line that spoke of Jimmy's difficulties stemming from a 'neuropsychological basis,' and the one about 'Obsessive-Compulsive' behavior. I was still trying to digest the use of the term 'learning disabilities'.

I was confused. My son has an average IQ. He is intelligent. How many kids know their ABCs before they are two? He knows so many things. This does not fit the profile of someone who is learning disabled?! I was frustrated. Jim and I rode down the creaky old elevator in silence. Our neat little plan of tidying up all Jimmy's problems by the time school started in the fall was shot to the moon. We held hands as we silently walked to the parking garage. After a quick parting kiss, and a promise that we'd discuss everything when he got home, Jim walked towards his car, and I towards mine.

6

Reality Check

Jim seemed withdrawn when he arrived home from work that evening. 'I need to read the report again,' he said after dinner. He went into the den, sat at his desk and silently pored over the report one more time. During the day, I had shared the report with his mother and had faxed a copy to my parents. Their responses were supportive, but tinged with an underlying sadness at the news it contained. After the kids were tucked into bed, Jim and I watched the late news in silence, and then retired to bed.

'I just don't see how she can write him off like that,' Jim said in the darkness. We pulled the covers up to our chins to ward off the February chill.

'You mean the psychologist?'

'Uh huh,' he said. 'She's telling us that he'll never hold a high skilled job and never go to college. I think she's full of crap.'

'Are you sure?' I asked. 'Did she really say all that?' I wondered what I had missed of the conversation.

'I just don't understand how she can give him a few tests and write him off, just like that!' Jim said with frustration. 'I just don't understand it. Jimmy is so smart, and so bright.'

'I'm just as thrown by this as you are,' I said. 'I just can't believe that a child as smart as Jimmy has a learning disability. It just doesn't make sense.'

'She's telling us to forget college and sign him up for vocational courses. Echo, he's only a five-year-old!'

'I didn't hear her say that.'

'You were in the same room, weren't you?'

'Well I did have to leave and go to the bathroom. Maybe I missed something?' I pulled the blanket up over my shoulder – wondering. Did I miss something? Or was this a gender gap scenario. I saw the cup as half full. Jim saw the cup as half empty. After all, I mused, our opinions never agreed on a movie that we had seen together, or how high on the wall to hang a picture; what made me think that we would emerge with the same perceptions of our visit with the psychologist?

Jim turned over and punched his pillow, which signaled his three-minute countdown until he was asleep – a skill which I greatly envied. I often lay awake for at least 30 minutes before I could relax enough to go off into La-La Land.

'Well, we can listen to her up to a point,' I said. 'But we don't have to accept this notion of limiting his potential.'

'You're damn right we don't.'

'So we'll get him the help he needs for the next couple of years and then everything will be fine.'

As he drifted off to what would be a troubled sleep, I wondered about the years ahead. It seemed like the more help we got, the more problems were presented to us. I had never known anyone with a learning disability. Jimmy had a wealth of knowledge stored up inside that little brain of his. He had an amazing ability to memorize things. Granted, he was 'unique' in his way of interacting with others. All he needed was help in learning to be less aggressive and to express his feelings. This does not prohibit him from attending college! Maybe Jim was right. The report was pretty dismal. I didn't want to write Jimmy off any more than my husband. Did I have a view of the world that was less jaded than my husband's? Was I the one in denial?!

When Jim and I got married, the Bishop who married us gave us the advice that we should look at each day as an 'adventure'. We've often remembered his advice. The night we sold our house and were staying in a hotel during our move to New Jersey was one of those 'adventure' experiences. The hotel didn't have a crib for Jimmy, so we put him in between us on the bed. At three o'clock in the morning, Jimmy hit the floor with a thud. His screams must have been loud enough to wake all the hotel guests on the floor. As I soothed my frightened child, Jim groggily asked in the darkness, 'Are we having an adventure yet?' We both started laughing. The question has become a sort of mantra in our marriage when things turn for the worse.

I guess we are having another one of those adventures. Under the pillow, I gave Jim's hand a little squeeze. He sleepily squeezed back. With a silent prayer of thanks for the good man lying next to me, I finally drifted off. Rest was a welcome relief from the day's events.

Deanie called me within a few days. We had authorized the release of the psychological report and she had just finished reading it. Now was the time to get together and develop a plan for Jimmy. Kindergarten was coming up in the fall. We had to decide if we wanted to place him in a public school, or try to find a private school. Since he would be turning six in the summer, the law said we had to place him in an educational setting. We could not opt to wait out another year or we'd have the authorities knocking on our door. The first question I had was whether or not I should take Jimmy to the neighborhood school for the routine assessment. It was a mandatory thing for all incoming students to participate in a basic skills screening.

'You are going to have to do that anyway if you decide to go with the public school,' said Deanie, who indicated that it wouldn't hurt to take Jimmy over there. We could always decide for private school placement later.

We arrived at the neighborhood school on the screening day. The auditorium was filled with dozens of five-year-olds, many (as we were) accompanied by younger siblings. The acoustics in the room were hardly friendly. I grimly wondered what the decibel-level was like during the lunch hour. Jimmy immediately covered his ears and refused to take off his coat. Although he was uncomfortable, he was clearly happy to be inside the 'big-boy' school.

The testing was done on the stage at the front of the auditorium. Jimmy, hands still covering his ears, managed to get away from me while I was talking with one of the PTA mothers. He swaggered out onto the stage apron, extended one arm, (with his shoulder still covering that ear) and proceeded to give some sort of speech, no doubt from one of the videos he's glommed on to. He was distracting the kids who were taking their tests on the stage. I immediately recognized the looks of annoyance from some of the test examiners and hurried up there to yank him off the stage.

Later, when it was Jimmy's turn to take the assessment, he was barely able to concentrate on the tasks at hand. He was so focused on the fact that he was on the stage. I had to keep reminding him to pay attention to the tester.

'What a stage ham he is,' commented the tester cheerfully. 'He'll be great in the school play.'

'He certainly is,' I responded, my mind going back to the time I call 'The Grocery Store Incident.' Jimmy was a three-year-old and was very much into a series of religious videos. Our family all belongs to the Church of Jesus Christ of Latter-Day Saints, more commonly known as the Mormons. One of the videos details the Book of Mormon story of Christ's visit to the indigenous people of the American continent. Jimmy had watched this one until he knew every line of the video by memory.

On this particular day, I had both the kids with me and we were buying a rather large order of food at the local grocery store. I had two grocery carts filled. Jimmy was sitting in one, Caroline in the other. I had spent the better part of two hours navigating two overstuffed grocery carts through the store's aisles.

As I busily unloaded my groceries at the check-out line, Jimmy managed to unlatch the little safety belt on his shopping cart, stood up, outstretched his arms and said in a small, yet very clear voice, 'Behold, I am Jesus Christ.'

The busy activity suddenly came to a halt. My mind raced to that old television commercial about E.F. Hutton, the Wall Street brokerage firm. 'When E.F. Hutton speaks, (the action stops and everyone turns to hear...) everybody listens.' The young grocery bagger looked at my son as though he were a blasphemer. Disgust was evident on his face. The thought briefly crossed my mind of taking one kid under each arm and bolting for the door, but I had a couple of hundred in groceries sitting there that I had worked two hours to assemble.

'Jimmy, SIT DOWN!' I said firmly. 'Nobody wants to hear the "Sermon on the Mount" today.' I wasn't going to bother to explain the theological basis of his declaration. We already looked like religious zealots anyway.

'I've really got to cut down on his TV time,' I muttered to the cashier as I signed the check, took my groceries and my 'embarrassment' out the door.

Yes, Jimmy was certainly a ham. As I chatted with the tester, I could sense that Jimmy most likely bombed the screening for Kindergarten. She was not allowed to give any indications to the parents of the test results during that day, but I could read a hint of 'our people will be calling you for a follow-up' expression on her face. It was to be expected. I would have been surprised if Jimmy had passed the screening.

I turned around to see Jimmy at the front of the stage, his arm raised in what I like to describe as the 'Caesar pose'. He had managed to attract a small gaggle of kids and was loving it. Other mothers stood off to the side of the room, looking at the scene. I wondered if they thought he was just acting 'cute' or if their comments to each other about my son's antics carried a more nasty tone. I breathed a sigh of resignation and walked forward to collect him. I smiled weakly at my neighbors as I tried to grab Jimmy, who was pretending to be 'Mr. Conductor' from the *Thomas the Tank*

Engine TV show. The neighbors smiled back. When Jimmy saw that I meant business and that it was time to leave that wonderful stage, he collapsed into a lump of flesh. I was not going to try and negotiate with my son as he lay there in front of the whole neighborhood, school staff, and any other passers-by – watching to see how I would handle Jimmy's silent show of defiance. I simply picked him up, threw him over my shoulder like a sack of potatoes, and exited stage left in humiliation.

Such embarrassments were common. Jimmy could be so unpredictable. During the younger years, people thought he was just bright and saucy when he would tell a stranger they had bad breath. As he grew older, the 'cuteness' of his precocity wore off and strangers regarded him as annoying. Shaking off such instances of public humiliation was not only a skill I would have to learn, but Jim and, later, Caroline would as well. As much as we worked with our son to teach him the rules of proper social deportment, the stares, snickers, and spiteful comments would all become occupational hazards when going out in public with Jimmy. It would amaze me how some will freely offer their opinions on corporal punishment with no regard for the feelings of the parent, or knowledge of the child's situation. 'If you'd just give that kid a good spank, he'll shape up right quick,' they'd say.

The memory of my son's antics would quickly leave the minds of those strangers who made their opinions known. But their messages would often haunt me for days. It was even worse when such comments would come from a friend or family member. Early on, I learned that I had to let these things roll off or I would be dragged down emotionally. My family could ill afford to have this happen. I had a choice. I could be in control of how I felt, or I could let the thoughtless barbs eat my insides out.

I had scheduled a consultation with Deanie so we could map out a plan for the rest of the year. We had to decide what type of school was best for Jimmy, and I had to learn the ropes on procedure. If a child is enrolled in special education at a public school, there is a maze of rules, regulations, and an underlying culture that I had to be educated on. I couldn't simply turn my child over to the authorities and trust that they would make the best decisions for him. According to Deanie, it was a game of cat and mouse. Parents were often never told such services were available. It was up to the parent to do the research, scratch for information, and hound the authorities for every single service that the child got.

'I feel like I am walking into the lion's den,' I quipped to Deanie. I had started networking with parents of special needs children, attending local meetings of the Learning Disabilities Association. The war stories I heard were enough to curl my hair. I was horrified by the treatment that some parents and students had received. It was enough to scare me away from the public school venue and look immediately towards private schools. To hear these parents talk, there was no possible way the public schools could help my child.

I was overwhelmed. It was like going to work for a new company, where you didn't know the rules, the corporate culture, and where one single faux-pas can ruin the 'career' of your child.

'You *do* have to look at this like a job, said Deanie. 'You are going to be dealing with professionals, and so you will have to approach your interaction with the schools as a professional. The most important thing to remember is that *you are the expert* on your child. The hardest thing you'll do is to check your emotions at the door when you meet with the school authorities.'

I was wide-eyed; furiously scribbling notes on education law. Deanie cautioned me to keep detailed notes on all my phone calls, meetings and communications with the school officials. I felt pretty naive. What was I getting myself into? Deanie counseled me to take Jim to all the meetings because as sexist as it sounds, fathers are taken more seriously than the mothers.

Over the next few weeks, Deanie found me a couple of leads on local private schools that might be a good match for Jimmy. After consulting with Jim, I started the first round of phone calls. I was nervous, wondering what kinds of questions I would ask. In all honesty, I felt that I had no clue what I was doing. All I could do was work off my 'mother gut'. I figured I would know the right place when I saw it.

I visited a few schools. Although they seemed nice, I never got the feeling that they were the right place to send Jimmy. I felt like Goldilocks, sitting in the tiny chairs that seem to abound at all the schools. One had too many kids in the class, the other was situated in a building that was too near a busy street. Jimmy would never be able to pay attention with the 18-wheeled-trucks zooming past his classroom window all day. One school looked good, but the tuition costs were too steep. Another was a 30-minute ride from the house. During the whole search process, I never walked into a place where I felt at 'home'.

After several weeks of searching, I spoke to Deanie and told her that I felt ambivalent about all the schools I had visited. There was nothing out there that was setting me afire. I guessed that I would have to break down and see what the public schools were like. I was scared to death.

'You'll be fine,' she said. 'You are going with your gut and that's the best way to handle this situation.'

In April, my husband and I telephoned our local school to make an appointment to see the principal. According to the law, we must first write up a letter requesting services for our child. We attached a copy of Jimmy's psychological evaluation as proof that such an evaluation is warranted, and requested in writing that a formal evaluation be conducted by the authorities in our school district. According to Deanie, this was the only way we would get Jimmy the services that he needed. The visit to the principal's office was not necessary, but according to Deanie, it sent a message that Jimmy Fling had two concerned parents who would not let their son slip through the cracks. The visit lasted all of ten minutes. We chatted, signed the necessary papers, and left.

Over the course of the next few weeks, I received several phone calls and letters from the officials. They had assigned a manager to 'my case' and this person had invited me to visit several classroom placements to help determine the appropriate setting for Jimmy. I was pleased. This wasn't the kind of attitude that I had been warned about at the monthly LDA meetings.

My first visit was to a regular education Kindergarten classroom at the neighborhood school. The classroom was brightly decorated, with the children's artwork and other seasonal graphics hanging on the wall. The teacher was a kind, quiet-voiced woman. Along with the case manager, I watched the morning's activities from teeny-tiny chairs. I made a mental note to forego a skirt and opt for pants on all these classroom visits.

Despite the nurturing teacher, I couldn't help but have the niggling feeling that this was a wrong environment for Jimmy. My gut instinct told me the brightly-colored walls would be a distraction. Jimmy would be more attracted to the decorations and spend less mental energy listening to the teacher. I had also heard that enrollment projections were predicting that Jimmy's class would have 25 pupils. This figure was way too high. Jimmy would daydream his school day away and fall through the cracks. Ultimately, he needed a small class setting with a nurturing teacher. Did it exist?

A week later, the case manager took me to visit another classroom in a school across town. This was a program for children who had multi-handicaps, she explained, and might be an appropriate placement for Jimmy, depending on how his test results come in on the school's screening. The teacher had an excellent reputation, a fact that I had heard independently in my networking around town. She was a large, jolly woman, whose forte was structure. Although she didn't come off as the nurturing type, the kids loved her. I still came away cold. The class size was smaller, but I didn't feel the other students would be a match for Jimmy. They were loud and unpredictable, and the commanding voice of the teacher was something Jimmy wasn't ready for. He would certainly put his fingers in his ears at the sound of her voice! We were getting closer to what I was looking for, but I still wasn't there.

Later that month, I visited a classroom and found it all. It took me less than three minutes to feel that this was 'it'. The case manager had taken me to a classroom for children who were communication handicapped. The class size was small and the teacher was perfect, and the children were quiet and well behaved. The classroom had a slightly muted quality to it, which appealed to me. The window shades were drawn nearly all the way so as to limit outside distraction. The teacher was a slight, soft-spoken woman who used a great deal of language learning in her teaching methods, and structure in the children's schedule.

'I told you that "I'd know it when I saw it,"' I said to the case manager as we left the building. 'In my mind, this is the right classroom situation for Jimmy.' I listed all the things that I saw and gave the rationale for my observations.

She cautiously agreed with me, adding that we must wait for the results of Jimmy's screening before anything can be final. This frustrated me, but I felt a sense that all would be well in the end.

Over the course of the next several months, Jim and I had written off the idea of private school and were banking on the public school setting. After what I had seen of the communication handicapped classroom, I was sold on the idea that they could give Jimmy the appropriate education, despite the public school naysayers that I had heard up to that point. The screening was to take place in July, the day after we returned from our family vacation. When I mentioned this to my network of LDA friends, they chided me for letting 'them' push back the date of the testing for so many weeks. The school was required by law to do the screening within a certain time period. I didn't see what the big deal was. I knew that year-end for the school was very busy. All of the authorities had to do the paperwork on students already in the system. Why push myself in at a time that is inconvenient? I could have insisted that they follow the law to the letter, but what purpose would it serve? It would only aggravate the very people that I was trying to build a relationship with.

On the appointed test day, I arrived at the school with Jimmy and Caroline. The psychologist was going to give Jimmy a few tests, and I was to meet with the social worker. I was more than nervous. A social worker!

To my relief, the main topic of conversation was Jimmy and how I saw his needs. 'Jimmy has a very hard time communicating his thoughts,' I said. 'Unless you have the benefit of seeing his favorite video, you rarely have any idea of what he is trying to say.' I re-told the social worker the 'Mama is a snowblower' story. I described how Jimmy had trouble organizing his thoughts enough to get the communication out of his mouth. 'By the time he gets it clear in his mind what he wants to say, the rest of the world is two conversation topics ahead,' I said. 'Or worse, he takes too long and totally breaks down altogether and forgets what it was he was thinking about in the first place.' I told the social worker that this makes it very hard for him to carry on a normal conversation with other children, who are much, much quicker with things like this. Then I asked her to make sure she said in her report that he needed directions repeated more than once. 'Whoever his teacher is will need a huge amount of patience.' The meeting went very well and I left with the realization that social workers didn't just deal with those in crisis situations.

At the end of the month, we received a phone call to meet with the school authorities. They had the results of the testing and Jimmy's scores indicated that a placement in special education was warranted. My mind was a mixture of relief and sadness. I was happy that Jimmy would qualify for the services that he needed. His communication skills deficits and weakness in fine motor skills were sufficient reason to place him in a special class. At the same time, I was sad that my son officially had a label: communication handicapped.

Before school started, I began preparing Jimmy for the big transition. He would be gone all day to school, would ride the bus across town, and face a host of other changes to his normal routine. He would not have his beloved morning dose of 'Public Television'. He would be physically separated from me for the entire day. Up to this point, his longest stretch away from home was the three hours he was at the preschool. The demands of school and classwork would be intense. He was not used to such demands being made on him for an entire day. His whole life was about to change and everything was going to be NEW, NEW, NEW! New teachers, new kids, new building to go to, new bus to ride, new lunchbox, new clothes to wear, new backpack to remember – new everything! I was afraid that he would balk at all the changes. It only made sense to me that I should expose him to as much of his new routine as possible.

Jimmy had received a welcome letter from his new teacher. I was disappointed that he was not assigned to the same school building or teacher that I had seen earlier that spring. I had no idea about the new school building he was assigned to. Who knows what kind of teacher he would be assigned to now! By that time, the point was moot. I had heard through the grapevine that the lovely teacher I had met earlier that year had gone out on maternity leave. I had to trust on blind faith that the placement was the same as the one I saw earlier that Spring.

I knew from my friends in the neighborhood that all the teachers had to report to the school several days ahead of the start date to set-up their classrooms and prepare for the Fall term. I made arrangements to take Jimmy to visit his new school and meet his teacher. When the day arrived, Jimmy held tightly to my hand as we entered the front door of the school. The halls were quiet except for the sound of the janitorial staff polishing the floors. We stopped by the main office, announced ourselves, and asked to see the new teacher. A woman directed us to a classroom down the hall.

'You must be Jimmy,' said the new teacher, who to my delight, had 'nurture' written all over her face. I was ecstatic! Jimmy's teacher had a slight build, coming nearly up to my chin in height. She had facial features that were strikingly similar to a young woman we had recently hired as a baby-sitter. Jimmy warmed up to her immediately. She showed him the classroom, invited him to select the desk that he wanted, and let him open the door to see the bathroom facilities. We chatted amiably for several minutes and Jimmy and I left to go see the play area. I had a good feeling about the new school and the teacher. My gut was telling me that we had made the correct decision for Jimmy.

7

Away at School

The first day of school had come. Like any mother who was sending her firstborn off to school, my feelings of excitement were tinged with a sense of sadness at the prospect of letting the first little one out of the nest. Deep in the back of my mind, my heart hurt because I would not be walking my son to school as would the rest of the neighborhood mothers who had children starting Kindergarten that day. My son would be picked up in a special school transportation van. I had heard that some of the kids in the neighborhood called these vans the 'retard bus'. As much as you paint a happy face on the situation, the reality of the whole scenario never completely leaves the subconscious. The simple fact that your child has a special van come to the house each school day lets the whole world know that he has some kind of disability. Any privacy you might want to keep is blown to smithereens. Questions were asked, not only by the neighbors, but by Jimmy too. He wanted to know why he wasn't going to the same school as the rest of the kids in the neighborhood. How do you tell a six-year-old just how complicated his life has become?!

As soon as the questions started coming, I resolved to answer each as straightforwardly and honestly as I could. I figured if I educated the neighbors to Jimmy's disability, the more sensitive they could be to his needs. The first steps in public awareness begin at home. Interestingly, it was Caroline who had more questions about the whole issue of school placement.

'Why isn't Jimmy going to school with Mike?' she asked.

I was startled by her question. My little Girly, who talked so much that you wanted to muzzle her, yet never probed with life's more difficult questions, had suddenly shown that she had been paying close attention to the happenings over the last several months.

'Mommy and Daddy have been looking for the right school for your brother,' I said. 'We wanted to make sure it has the best teachers for Jimmy.' My answer seemed to satisfy her three-year-old mind for the present time. I knew more questions would come later.

I got out the video camera to document the momentous occasion. Jimmy wore a black 'Batman' T-Shirt and a pair of gray shorts. He was ready with his small blue backpack. The school van pulled up and stopped in front of the house. With the camera running, Jimmy, Caroline, and I walked across the street.

'Are you Jimmy?' called the driver from the window. 'My name is Helen. Are you ready to go to school today?'

The doors swung open. Jimmy could hardly wait to board the bus. Helen reminded Jimmy to wave good bye, which he did with a perfunctory swoop of his arm. He found his seat and never looked back. The doors swung shut and the van rolled to the corner, stopped for traffic, and drove away. As I caught it all on camera, I thought with a bit of irony of the times many years before, that I had wielded a video camera collecting tape for news broadcasts. Today, I was capturing an event that was much more important.

As I relished the moment, I began to hear a whimpering at my feet. I panned down with my camera to catch Caroline's distress at the sight of her brother's school van going around the corner. She covered her face with her hands and started to sob.

'What's the matter, Girly?' I asked.

'I'm gonna miss Jimmy,' came the tiny muffled voice between sobs. She grabbed my left thigh and broke down. 'I'm gonna miss my brother.'

That got to me. I wanted to be a three-year-old again and sit down on the curb with her and let it all hang out. I started to choke up, but decided quickly that I wasn't going to let her see my distress. She started preschool the next day and I wanted it to be all sunshine and roses.

'You know what?' I said. 'I'll bet Jimmy has a really good time at school.' My voice was trailing off into a whisper. I could barely speak, hoping Caroline was too distraught to notice. Shutting off the camera, we went back into the house. After distracting Caroline with some activities, I went into the laundry to sort wash. Like all the other mothers who had sent their children away to school for the first time, I joined the sniffling sisterhood by crying five full minutes into my soiled tea towels. I gave birth and had so earned this rite of passage. So what, that I had a large headache for the rest of the day! I was a mother!

Jimmy seemed to make the transition into the new school very well. He arrived home very tired, almost exhausted, but that was to be expected of any little one. Each day, he would bring home his backpack filled with papers. I saved every one, remembering Deanie's admonitions to save all paperwork and that of my new friends who told me to document everything. I kept all his papers piled in a large cardboard box.

In a few weeks' time, I received a phone call from the school. On the line was Debbie Dono, who would be working twice a week with Jimmy with his speech and language therapy. She had written up an education plan and needed me to come in and sign the paperwork so she could proceed with the work. This was the beginning of a parent–professional partnership that would last six years.

At first glance, I knew Jimmy would like working with Debbie. She was medium height, a slender build, and her dark hair framed her expressive brown eyes. Her voice carries just a trace of the accent of a native New Yorker, with a smile as big as the Long Island Sound. The most striking aspect of Debbie's personality is her enthusiasm for kids. Jimmy once described her as 'perky'. As I would come to learn later in our working relationship, Debbie's biggest asset is her ability to go with her intuition. Her success with Jimmy, in large part, was a result of her skills in receptivity, looking past the superficial and finding the deeper meaning.

Although she had never met Jimmy, Debbie's education plan was right on target. Her first item on the list was heavy emphasis on the social part of language, what the professionals call 'pragmatics'. Her goal was to teach Jimmy the basics of conversation, a simple 'hello' greeting, how to start a conversation, and how to maintain a conversation once it got going. Later in the year, she would advance to the 'WH' questions, which were a significant weakness for Jimmy in the screening test. It was very difficult for Jimmy to answer, Who, What, When, Where, and especially the Why questions. If she accomplished those two goals, we both decided it would have been a very successful year.

Debbie called me with a report after the first week's sessions with Jimmy. Apparently, things were going to have to be scaled back and taken very slowly. Jimmy wasn't ready just yet to get to work. He was still getting used to the idea of being at school every day.

'I brought him into my classroom and he sat down at the table,' said Debbie. 'We kind of looked at each other for a while and Jimmy's first words to me were, "I'm going to jump out of this window and run home to my mother."'

We both giggled. Debbie admitted that Jimmy's statement took her completely by surprise. He had always been a man of few words. I wondered which movie video Jimmy pulled that statement from. The interesting thing about the scene, according to Debbie, was Jimmy's lack of emotion about the whole thing. Most kids who wanted to get out of such a situation would have been screaming from the top of the roof. Jimmy, on the other hand, calmly mentioned that he was going to jump out a window and run home, just as if he were announcing he was going to check for mail in the postbox.

As it turned out, Debbie would have to spend the first month with Jimmy establishing a comfort level. She instinctively felt that Jimmy had a big need to feel 'safe' at school and in her classroom. She described the first few weeks with Jimmy as 'getting to know you' time. Taking a cue from Deanie, with whom she consulted frequently, Debbie brought out board games and played them with Jimmy. She reported to me her advances in teaching 'turn-taking' and keeping a conversation going. 'It's interesting how much direct teaching I have to do with Jimmy,' observed Debbie. 'I have to coach him in just about everything!'

Debbie was fascinated with how she was consistently scaling back her expectations in order to get to the business of teaching Jimmy the very core of communication. The things she thought were basic were actually too advanced for her new student. Although Jimmy was able to speak – at times very eloquently – on a certain TV show or movie video he was obsessed with, Debbie quickly realized that he did not have a handle on the things that most children take in naturally. Debbie had to plainly teach Jimmy about the back-and-forth of conversation; one person speaks, then the other. She had to teach him about listening to the words the other person was saying. Jimmy was taught that the only way to have a good back-and-forth conversation is to listen while the other person is talking. That way, he would know what would be good to say next.

Then there was the whole issue of eye contact and why it was important. Jimmy learned that the other person needs to feel like you are listening. Debbie told Jimmy this is accomplished through eye contact. She would take Jimmy around the halls at the school and the two would practice conversation with anyone who would walk their way. With their sessions three times a week, I soon realized the lessons were going rather well because darn near everyone at the school knew the intimate details of life at the Flings. One day

I visited the school and the school secretary asked, 'Is your house OK? I heard you burned your dinner last night.'

The whole thing was mind boggling for both Debbie and me. Up to this point, we thought all these little things just came naturally to everyone we knew. She quickly learned that the job of teaching these simple things was very complex. All the skills fell in the nonverbal realm. This was the biggest challenge for Debbie. How does one teach verbally about the nonverbal things that everyone takes in naturally?

At the time, there were no published instructional strategies available for her to draw from, so Debbie worked with Jimmy using her gut instinct.

At home, Jimmy was very non-communicative. It was frustrating for me, figuring that a day's worth of stimulation at school would generate conversation with my son. I would ask the typical mother-type questions like, 'How was your day?' I'd get no response. I knew that this was typical of kids, but the more I probed, and tried to elicit information in hopes of starting a conversation with my son, the more I realized that he genuinely did not know the answers to even the most basic questions. Even after several months of attending class, he still could not tell me the names of the other children!

I was invited to assist Jimmy's class as the 'room mother'. Each class had a parent representative who coordinated class parties and accompanied the children on day trips away from the school. I was more than happy to volunteer. It afforded me a glimpse into my son's life at school, so I could have some kind of contextual base when approaching him in conversation at home. It also allowed me access to the teachers at the school and because I needed to be a frequent visitor to the school, it allowed both the teachers and me to easily keep in constant communication about Jimmy's progress.

Over the course of the school year, it became evident that Jimmy was very homesick and missed me terribly. Yet, he was very un-emotional about letting me know his feelings. He would be putting his coat on, getting himself out the door, and would blithely tell me that he didn't want to go to school. He wanted to stay home with me and Caroline. I ignored his comments. How homesick could he really be if he was walking out the door at the same time he was telling me how much he missed me!? It just didn't make sense. I felt as though he was trying to manipulate me, and wasn't doing a very good job at it.

During the year, I kept in touch with the teacher and Debbie, and supplemented the classwork with work at home. Every opportunity was turned into a teaching moment. I was going to make my son the world's most socially aware person, even if it was going to kill me. My role was to be Jimmy's personal 'color commentator' on life. If I did it enough, I hoped that some of the information would sink into his brain.

The first rule in my mind, was to assume that Jimmy knew nothing – as if he had just arrived on a plane with a load full of penguins from Antarctica. I would have to point out the obvious social mores of life. One day, we got into the car and drove around the corner towards the store. On the way, we saw Mike, a boy in the neighborhood that Jimmy saw off-and-on, and whom he considered to be his friend.

'Look! There's Mike,' I'd say, tooting the horn. 'Look Jimmy, He's waving. You need to wave back.' Jimmy, of course, needed a couple of seconds to let the information sink in before he'd respond. Caroline, on the other hand, was practically hanging out the window at first mention, screaming Mike's name at the top of her lungs, waving furiously. I was constantly on the lookout for these kinds of teaching opportunities – like hunting for pennies on the sidewalk.

One of the things Deanie pointed out to me was Jimmy's lack of understanding about emotion. How do you teach emotion?! Isn't emotion something that everyone is supposed to understand and obtain through social osmosis? I already taught Jimmy to recognize facial expressions through the 'face game' that we played. But I sensed that things needed to go much deeper than that. Sure, he knew what the faces looked like, but he was only beginning to know what feelings they represented. This was illustrated to me one day when Caroline fell and hurt her knee.

'Look Jimmy, Girly's crying. She fell down and hurt her knee.' Jimmy just gave me a blank stare and put his fingers in his ears. 'Can you go help her up and tell her you're sorry that she feels sad?' Jimmy walked over and stood next to his sister, who by now had calmed herself. He looked at me, then at Caroline and said, 'A little less noise.'

Videos again! This time, Jimmy was mimicking Cyril Ritchard's classic portrayal of George Darling/Captain Hook in the 1960s American television production of *Peter Pan*. Jimmy watched it to the point where the dialog was burned into his brain. I couldn't help but laugh. Jimmy had it down pat – right down to mimicking Ritchard's condescending tone. I had my work cut out for me.

The thought occurred to me that if Jimmy's videos provided context to his world, then it might prove useful to use them as a teaching tool. One of Jimmy's obsessions was the *Thomas the Tank Engine* television series. It played every day on the American public television network and Jimmy could set his internal clock to the time the show appeared. It was a daily ritual. He taped most of the episodes with the video recorder. The show's first season had Ringo Starr playing the part of Mr. Conductor. When George Carlin took over the role in 1992, Jimmy suddenly stopped watching the show. He was angry about the change in casting. 'This is not right anymore!' he protested in a huff. It was several months before he would watch it again. I was surprised by the depth of his anger and it took me a while to figure out that the reason he stopped watching it was because Ringo got replaced with another actor. My husband dryly commented that he didn't know his kid was such a big Ringo fan.

Jimmy had insisted that I buy each one of the little metal train engines when they became available in the stores. It seemed like every month, a new one was introduced. I cringed because Jimmy was insistent that he own each and every one of those engines. I recall one time, I desperately searched in three states for 'Bill and Ben'. Jimmy was incapable of getting his mind off the little engines. Literally obsessed with the thought of them. When one was purchased, he fixated on another. Like a dog with a bone, Jimmy wouldn't, or couldn't, let go of the idea. He had some kind of desperate need to possess each one of the engines. He would pester me for them until I wanted to scream. The first thing he would say in the morning was, 'When are we going to get Ben and Bill?' He just wouldn't be satisfied until he had the next engine in his hand. He would line them all up and lie down on the floor and just stare at them from eye level. Or at times, he would pick one up and examine it from every possible angle. Jimmy didn't play with the little engines in the normal sense, he just spent an inordinate amount of time gazing at them.

Some of my friends thought I was nuts to go to such lengths to buy a silly, small train engine – and even said so. Those who thought I was excessively indulgent of my son just didn't understand the predicament. Jimmy HAD to have those engines. He was driven to distraction with thoughts of them. To preserve my sanity and keep peace in the home, I spent the few dollars and got the engines that he wanted.

One afternoon, I took all the engines and lined them up on the kitchen table. When I knew Jimmy would be nearby, I feigned an interest in them, hoping to catch his interest too. The whole process is like fishing. I had the bait, the lure and was just waiting for my little fish to come swimming by. It didn't take long before I had set the hook and I was reeling him in.

'Which one is Thomas?' I asked. Jimmy picked up the little blue engine. The paint was beginning to show wear. The adhesive sticker that made up the face was starting to peel. Later, the sticker would fall off and Jimmy would insist that I buy another Thomas.

'Do you remember when Thomas crashed into the pile of snow? I asked. Jimmy made a sad face. 'What kind of a face are you showing me?' I probed.

'Sad face,' Jimmy offered.

'That's right. Thomas started to cry when the snow covered up his wheels, didn't he.'

'Oh my wheels and coupling rods!' murmured Jimmy.

I knew he had the mental picture of the episode where the little train has an accident and plows right into a snowbank. The dialog was matching perfectly. I decided to make a connection.

'Do you remember when Caroline fell down and hurt her knee this afternoon?' Jimmy nodded. 'She cried, didn't she, just like Thomas.' I waited for his gray matter to finish churning.

'Did Girly feel sad just like Thomas?' he asked.

'Yes, she did.' I answered evenly. Inside my pulse was racing. He was getting it and I didn't want to distract from the issue with my excitement. I took the next step.

'Do you remember that Terrance the Tractor came to help Thomas out of the snow? That was a nice thing to do. It made Thomas feel better, didn't it?' I waited to see the little Bingo light flash inside his mind.

'Mom?' he asked after a few moments of staring at the trains. 'Do you want me to help Caroline like Terrance helped Thomas?'

'Yes, that would be the right thing to do.' I was giddy. This must be the feeling a teacher has when a student finally grasps a concept! 'Helping people like Terrance did makes a sad person happy. You can help many people, even grown-ups.' Jimmy continued to gaze at the little train he held in his hand. The short window of opportunity had passed. Jimmy's attention was gone now. I was happy with this small advance. The true test of whether my impromptu lesson was a success would be to see if Jimmy could apply what he had been taught at a later time.

Spurred on by the advance, I began teaching Jimmy at every opportunity at home, and even out in public too. When we were at the grocery store, I would point out what seemed obvious to most. For Jimmy, these observations were lessons in managing his environment.

'Jimmy,' I would say in the soda aisle. 'See the red bottles of Coca Cola? Can you put two bottles of Coca Cola in my cart please?' I would let him push the cart up and down the aisles if the store wasn't too crowded.

'Jimmy, you need to watch out for the other customers. See the lady in the blue coat? When you move the cart near to her, you'll have to say, "Excuse Me" before you pass.'

Jimmy would always comply. Reactions from the fellow shoppers were mixed. Some thought he was adorable, the perfect gentleman. Others, usually men, would give me a withering look, their expressions silently saying, 'Mother, give the kid a break. He's old enough to already know this kind of stuff.' I was giving Jimmy a commentary on his world, pointing out emotions, feelings, and reactions with the hope that he would generalize the information and be able to use it within the context of his own life.

I continued to receive reports from Jimmy's teacher and Debbie about his progress at school. They were very concerned. Jimmy was still not making any social contacts in the class or at recess, and still didn't know the other children's names. Once he referred to another student as 'the black boy', which confused everyone because the child was of white ethnicity. Later it dawned on the staff that Jimmy was talking about the color of the boy's shirt.

Jimmy was very fearful and often kept his fingers in his ears at the slightest sound. We had his ears tested again and the results were inconclusive. During the fall, the school had invited a presenter in for a school assembly on astronomy. Part of the program featured a walk-in bubble that illustrated all the constellations. There was music and the lights were turned off. Jimmy was panic stricken. He would not go into the room where the assembly was being held. A teaching assistant had to sit outside in the hall with him. Lunch times were a waste, his food often going uneaten because his fingers were in his ears, or he would simply stare off into space.

The teachers were also concerned by the onset of Jimmy's self-stimulatory activities. They described the 'stimming' as both external and internally driven. He had recently started humming to himself and playing with imaginary toys. The teacher could not give him tokens or counters during math because he would just turn them into toys. 'He just seems so far away,' they said. 'As if he's on another planet.'

Even though I heard all these reports from the teachers, I remained unconcerned. Jimmy was just a little boy who was getting adjusted to his new routine at school. As far as his day dreaming; I was a world-class daydreamer in school too. I remember looking out the window during my high school biology class and trying to figure out how many times the 'Taco-Time' sign rotated during a one-minute period. Once I figured out how many times the restaurant's sign spun around, I would monitor the number of rotations to see if the gears functioned on a consistent level. The distraction provided me with a way to escape the dull monotony of the lecture. I was on another planet too. I got a 'B' in Biology and I turned out OK.

In hindsight, I was listening to the school officials but I wasn't hearing them. Jimmy was rapidly slipping away. Compared to his peers at school, Jimmy was obviously behind developmentally, and from all accounts, he was going further and further into a world of his own. I didn't see this kind of pulling away at home and wasn't as concerned as the teachers were. It would take an emotional sledge hammer to finally get me to understand the quicksand we were standing in.

8

Just a Lonely Boy

My husband likes to wash the cars on the weekend and this particular Saturday was no exception. I was outside with the children as they played in the front yard; continually warning them away from the spray of the hose my husband was wrestling with. Kids and water are like magnets. Sometimes it's just useless to fight and one has to just let the kids get wet.

The neighbors next door had recently gotten a new dog. The puppy was a female Collie mix, a very playful and inquisitive dog that barked quite a lot. Like most puppies, the dog frequently ran amok until the owners could corral it and take it back into the house. Jimmy didn't care for the new addition to the neighborhood. The barking drove him indoors, his hands over his ears.

That afternoon, Caroline was playing in a pile of dirt near where my husband was washing his sports car. I was on the front porch with Jimmy, who nervously eyed the dog playing in the yard next door. Suddenly the puppy bounded happily over to our yard and put both paws up on little Caroline's shoulders. My daughter was overwhelmed. Between barks, the dog started licking Caroline's face. It was all too much. She froze in place and began to scream hysterically. In her little mind, the dog was attacking her. My husband raised his head over the car to see what the commotion was and saw the barking dog in his daughter's beyond-frightened face. For the first time in our marriage, I saw him go over the top.

He raced around the car and pulled the barking dog off Caroline, and dragged it by the collar back over to the neighbor's yard. The little neighbor girl, by this time, had noticed that the dog had caused some trouble and had run to fetch her mother. As I comforted my daughter, I sat speechless as Jim began yelling at the poor woman who lived next door about keeping her dog off our property. I had never seen my husband, who is normally so even-tempered, speak to anyone in such a tone. His anger was a product of his deep sense of protectiveness to his children and he felt as attacked as Caroline had. The sad part about this whole episode was the children witnessed the whole scene as well. It had a profound impact on both of them. It would be three years before my neighbors would allow their child to step foot inside our home again – a friendship that my children could ill afford to lose. More serious, this incident instilled a fear of dogs and other animals that would negatively impact my children's ability to form friendships, and our family's ability to freely visit friends and relatives who owned pets. For the next several years, whenever we would announce that we were going anywhere, the first question would be, 'Do they have a dog?' It would be five more years before Caroline or Jimmy could muster up the courage to pet another dog. From Jimmy's perspective, playing outside was now a dangerous activity, fraught with fear that 'a dog might come'.

From that day on, Jimmy would only play outside if I accompanied him, and much of his time in the fresh air was spent in the 'safety' high up in his beloved Mimosa tree. Sadly, at about this same time, the only other boy in the neighborhood who was Jimmy's age adopted a beautiful chocolate Labrador dog, which dashed any hopes of the boys forming a close friendship. The simple act of leaving the house each morning for the walk down the driveway to the bus now would require all of Jimmy's courage. Each school morning, he ran down the driveway with a wild fear in his eyes that reminded me of the news pictures I had seen out of Bosnia. The anxiety was evident on his face as he stood and waited for the arriving bus to come to a complete stop and permission granted by the driver to cross the street. For my son, the outside world *was* like a war zone. Instead of sniper fire, he feared an encounter with a dog, which in his mind, was just as dangerous. At the time, I underestimated the depth of Jimmy's internal anxiety. Later, I would learn to appreciate the *bravery* that he mustered each day just to leave the house. The physical and emotional toll it must have taken on him is still unimaginable to me.

Compounding this event was another tragedy in our town, the impact of which escaped no one. Only a few months after the dog incident, a local seven-year-old girl was raped and murdered by a neighbor, a man she knew and trusted. She was reported missing by her parents on a Saturday night and the authorities cracked the case the next day when the neighbor, who turned out to be a convicted rapist, led the authorities to the child's body in a county park less than two miles from our home. The community was outraged. Pink ribbons sprouted up all over the township in remembrance of the little girl who was murdered. It had a deleterious impact on all the children, not only my own. Both children and parents didn't feel safe in their own neighborhoods, children were reported to be sleeping with the lights on at night, neighbors were irrationally eyeing each other suspiciously, wondering if there were any concealed criminal history. The fluttering pink ribbons that streamed from every tree, utility pole, and mailbox served as a constant reminder of the child's murder, and a subliminal suggestion of what could just as easily have happened to any of us. It was hard for anyone to overcome the feeling of discomfort that permeated our town that year. It was so pronounced that I had even made the climate of fear a topic in one of my weekly newspaper columns. The gloomy mood was pervasive! There was no escaping it, and this only compounded Jimmy's fear of the outside world.

We had made some minor changes to Jimmy's speech and language therapy at school that year. Debbie Dono felt that he would benefit more from a group session rather than a one-on-one; and would increase his opportunities for socialization. It was decided that Jimmy would work twice a week in a group of no more than three children, and have one session per week alone with Debbie. One of the boys had some mild articulation problems and Debbie did some work with all the boys on their 'S' and 'L' sounds. She was surprised to see that the articulation drills improved Jimmy's skills in paying attention and in forming eye contact. Debbie found that the exercises she used, which involved having Jimmy focus his attention to his face in a mirror, then focus his attention to Debbie's face, took Jimmy one step further in his understanding facial expressions. Up to that point, Jimmy only understood that you look at someone's face when you are talking to them. As he learned to properly make his 'S' sounds, using the mirror technique, Jimmy learned that there was a *purpose, a reason, a benefit to be gained,* by looking at someone's face while talking to them. The articulation drills helped him to advance beyond the abstract. Now Jimmy was able to generalize this skill during all his conversations. It was an important breakthrough. The articulation drills were the first means of applying Jimmy's knowledge of facial expressions. Now the whole concept of eye contact in conversations made sense to him. He started paying attention.

Jimmy still needed help in his language skills. He wouldn't ever initiate a conversation. He never spoke at school (and rarely at home) *unless* he was spoken to first. Debbie's goal that year was to help Jimmy understand the basics of conversation. During their one-on-one sessions, Debbie continued to take Jimmy out of the classroom and out into the halls of the school. They would go and visit the secretary in the office and practice 'Hello' with eye contact. Then they would make the rounds to the nurse's office, the guidance counselor, the custodian, the cooks in lunch room or whomever they happened upon in the hallway.

What I found most interesting was the idea that Debbie had to get down to the very basic elements of communication with my son. I found it odd that she was teaching him the basics of 'hello'. 'Jimmy should already *know* this,' I thought to myself. 'Why was she having to teach it?' How can someone exist on this earth and not be able to pick up on this most basic of communication skills. Yet, my Jimmy had some kind of neurological block to this sort of thing. It was a puzzling thing to me, and was something that I found impossible to explain to those who questioned me on the specifics (or necessity) of Jimmy's work with a speech/language specialist. They'd assume that I meant that Debbie was teaching Jimmy small-talk, or 'cocktail party chit-chat'. No, it was more basic than that. 'She's teaching him how to talk,' which didn't make sense. Jimmy already knew how to talk. I avoided questions because I really couldn't explain something I really didn't fully understand myself.

Jimmy's first grade teacher was the same woman he had the first year, which was very comforting to me. Jim and I had always noticed that Jimmy would become very agitated and at times would become disorientated if things were changed. The teachers had noticed this at school as well. He seemed to be thrown off kilter if there was any kind of change in the school schedule, or seating arrangements. 'He is very resistant to change,' they wrote in his school reports.

If there was one thing I could count on with Jimmy, it was his consistency. He always insisted on wearing the same type of clothes every day. Lunch was always the same thing, day-in and day-out. What I would later learn was that Jimmy's preference for sameness at age six, would mushroom into problematic rigidity by age nine.

What concerned his teachers the most was Jimmy's inability to stay focused, or at attention for a sustained amount of time. 'He's so distracted,' his teacher said at the January parent conference. 'In all areas.' We had all just enjoyed a lovely two-week break for the Christmas holiday and I chalked it up to Jimmy needing extra time to 'get back in the groove'.

'I'm really worried about him,' said the teacher. 'He seems to be slipping away. I could always count on him being able to stay focused during story time, but now we practically have to hold his hand to keep him with us.'

The teacher went on to describe Jimmy's lack of social interaction. 'He's not making any friends at all,' she said. 'We're checking out in the play yard during lunch recess and he's always alone.' I was most disappointed to hear this, although I wasn't surprised. This was Jimmy's second year with the same group of students and he still could not tell me the names of the other kids in his class. I knew these kids fairly well from my interaction as the room mother. Whenever I would ask him about the others, I was greeted with a blank stare. In fact he often would blank out and stare off into space. The teacher told me that Jimmy had started the annoying habit of humming and singing to himself. She related a story of how the mainstream music teacher stopped her in the hall to ask why would Jimmy hum loudly during the class. She described how he made strange faces while staring off into the distance or would grab at imaginary objects in the air.

I understood this behavior. I was beginning to see it at home but I didn't find it too problematic. Of course, I wasn't trying to teach addition, or reading to such a distracted child. In hindsight, I was de-sensitized. Dr. Matthews had noted some quirks during her evaluation of Jimmy two years before and had referred him to the local hospital where we had him tested for seizures. It was an arduous affair, which required me to spend the whole night keeping Jimmy awake and giving him a dose of medication just before we left for the test the next morning. Half the test was administered while he was awake; the other was during sleep. Gloppy gook was used to stick the electrodes to my son's scalp. Jimmy was too zoned out on the medication to get agitated over the procedure. For me, the sight of my little boy with electrodes pasted all over his head was upsetting. Afterward, we were told the EEG was normal and no evidence of seizures was found. Diagnosis: my little guy was just a daydreamer. I was relieved yet at the same time I was frustrated. Another dead end.

But there was more to report from the teacher. 'He always seems nervous or worried about something,' she said. This came as a surprise to me. I had always thought that Jimmy liked to know what was going to happen – before it was going to happen. But the teacher was characterizing his behavior as a constant stress. It was like he couldn't get his mind off of certain thoughts. I called it persistence; she called it obsession. It was like Jimmy was a little boy who walked around with a rain cloud over his head. Was there going to be recess? When do we go to lunch? Why is 'that boy' sitting in the wrong seat? Is there another fire drill today? How do I get to the bus? I want to go home. There was a constant stream of worries inside this little boy's mind.

When these concerns about Jimmy's attention difficulties first surfaced in Kindergarten, we had gone back to our pediatrician to ask him what he thought about Jimmy's behaviors. The teachers seemed to think that Jimmy had a condition called Attention Deficit Disorder (ADD) and we wanted to talk through this possibility with our doctor. They had said that many children had been placed on the drug Ritalin with dramatic results. Through my network of friends, I located a group of parents who met monthly to talk about issues concerning ADD and I signed up for local seminars by professionals who were expert in treating and educating the child with ADD.

I scheduled an appointment with our pediatrician. Both Jim and I sat nervously in his office. The reports from the teacher were pretty dismal. It was as though they were describing a stranger. He seemed so impaired at school, yet at home he was a calm, relaxed, quiet child. Why was there such a discrepancy? For what had seemed like an eternity, we were looking for answers and never got them. How much of the problem for Jimmy was his weak processing skills and how much was the ADD, if that was what he had? It had been over a year and I had not yet been given an explanation of what exactly the school meant by 'Auditory Processing Delay' that was satisfactory to me. Anything I heard was murky and nebulous. I wanted to understand what was happening in my child's brain that made him so distant, so hard to read, and drew him away from the world around him. What was happening that made it so difficult for him to communicate and understand other's communication? Why didn't he know the other kids' names in class? What was going on inside his mind that made him afraid to go outside alone? There *had* to be a medical reason for all this yet I got no answers. No one could articulate to me what was happening in my son's head that caused him to act so oddly. The only thing they wanted to talk about were his behaviors. The use of Ritalin was discussed and the doctor was reluctant to diagnose ADD. We were given a referral to a well-known pediatric neurologist in the area.

'Do you mean we just shelled out $45 for a consultation just so we could hear pediatrician say that he didn't know? — And now we're being sent to specialist who *might* know,' muttered Jim on the way home. He was as frustrated as I. Weren't doctors supposed to know all the answers? Were we expecting too much? Why couldn't anyone help us fix our problem?!

I placed a call to the neurologist's office and got the directions. The drive would take an hour. The appointment would be after work hours as this was the only way that Jim could join us. On the appointed evening, I loaded the kids into the car and started down the road. I was nervous and jumpy, my mind on several things. What if Jimmy had something other than ADD? What if the diagnosis was worse? What if the doctor didn't know? That would be the worst news of all. It had been three years of bumping around, going from specialist to specialist, and not getting all the answers about my son. I hoped that all my answers would be tied up in a nice little package with this neurologist.

We arrived at the office. To my relief, Jim was already waiting in the parking lot. Our eyes locked in a gaze which said it all: 'Are we having an adventure?' I checked in with the receptionist and was given a ream of forms to fill out. Names, birth dates, social security numbers, health history, work numbers, employer's address, insurance company number – you go blind filling out the forms. Every new specialist has their own set of forms they want you to complete. I finally got smart and kept cards with all the information on them in the wallet of my purse.

It had been a long day and we were all tired, especially Jimmy, who had been at school all day. A TV set in the corner kept the kids entertained while we waited. When Jimmy's turn came, the doctor called him into the examining room. Jim and I got up to accompany him but were turned away. The doctor wanted no distractions. We both looked at each other as we returned to our seats. 'He's the doctor,' I said.

After a 20-minute wait, we were called in to speak with the doctor. He validated the school's concerns saying, 'difficulties had been noted,' and he had noticed 'some distractibility' during the course of his neurological testing. However, all the tests came out normal. He described Jimmy as 'neurologically intact.' Translated: He didn't think our son had ADD, 'although there may be some element of a learning disability' what specifically, he couldn't say. He noted a mild bit of Scoliosis, which is a curvature of the spine, and suggested that we have a periodic orthopaedic screening done to monitor this. 'No medications are necessary.'

As we drove home, I felt a mixture of anger and confusion. After a quick 20-minute visit, how can this professional say that my child does not have an Attention Deficit!? *Or any other kind of problem?* 'Some element of learning disability?' Could he be more specific? My kid's teachers are telling me he is in 'La-La Land'. They have to physically touch him several times an hour just to get him to complete his schoolwork and to listen when he is being taught. How can this *not* be ADD? How can we walk out of here without any answers and with no diagnosis! I was steamed. We'd just taken another ride on the medical merry-go-round only to come up without any definitive answers. Another dead end.

There was nothing Jim or I could do but sit and watch our son fall further into a black hole. We had exhausted all our medical options. Everywhere we turned, the doctors kept saying Jimmy was normal. Where else could we go? We thought we'd knocked on every door imaginable! After five years of having our concerns for our son systematically invalidated, the feelings of self-doubt started creeping in. 'The doctors are probably all thinking we're making this stuff up,' I wailed to Jim on one particularly dismal evening. In hindsight, we had made the mistake of searching for all our answers in the field of medicine, when we should have gone back to the discipline of psychology, where ultimately, we would find our answer. Better yet, we should have gone to see a neuro-psychologist, and have had the benefit of both worlds.

The teachers were concerned. Jimmy's behaviors were getting worse. He was humming in class and making little chirping, odd noises. He still hadn't been able to socialize with the other children. It was taking the full attention of the teacher's aide to get Jimmy to stay focused and connected with the real world.

Eight months later, after Jimmy's teacher reported his symptoms had worsened, I took Jimmy back to the neurologist for a follow-up visit. He was concerned when I told him that the teacher had reported that Jimmy was humming during class, and he thought it was possibly a vocal tic. Why we never mentioned the humming during the first visit, I'll never know. I outlined for him the increased difficulty Jimmy was experiencing academically. I also told him about the significant problems he was having socially.

'He still doesn't know the names of the other kids in his class, and he's been with the same group for two years now,' I said. The doctor scribbled in the file. 'He also doesn't go outside to play very often. When he does go, he'll make a beeline for the tree and stay up there the whole time. The teachers say he doesn't play with any of the other kids at recess.'

'I recall that you wrote in your last report to us that Jimmy had friends. How did you come to that conclusion?' I casually mentioned, my heart pounding because I had never said anything to challenge a doctor in the past. They were all-knowing. One didn't question a doctor's methods and rationale.

The doctor said that he had asked Jimmy if he had friends, and of course, my son had said 'yes'. I wanted to smack the guy. How could he think that he would get accurate answers from a six-year-old with a communication handicap? That was the day I learned that doctors can and should be challenged. You have to give them more information than they ask for. Otherwise, they'll just make assumptions. The diagnosis of ADD was given. The doctor recommended that we consider the use of the drugs Ritalin or Clonidine, which he wouldn't prescribe. For *that*, we had to go back to our pediatrician.

'Well, the doctor says that Jimmy has ADD,' I reported to my husband after the visit.

'*Now* he says that?' was his skeptical response. 'What made the difference only eight months later?'

'I guess he got the whole story from me, rather than rely on our son for the details,' I groused, the 'friends' issue still hot in my memory. I was angry with the neurologist. Jimmy would have said yes to anything. If the doctor asked him if he was seeing things, Jimmy would have said 'yes'. It would have been the literal truth too because he would have 'seen' the doctor, the examining table, the nurse, and on and on and on!

Jim and I opted to table our discussion on the implications of the 'official' diagnosis of ADD. The hour was late, I had driven an hour home from the neurologist's office and it was time to put the kids to bed.

As was our custom, Jim put Caroline to bed and tucked her in. Like her father, she can drift off to sleep in less than three minutes. Jimmy's nightly ritual took much longer than his sister's did. Even though he was tucked into bed, he often lay awake for hours. Jim and I felt that if we kept the house quiet and let him alone, he would fall asleep, and often we would check on the children before retiring ourselves only to have his head pop up with an inquiring look. One night, I sat down next to him, started a late-night conversation, and was startled to find that Jimmy was quite chatty and lucid. He was in the mood to talk, and for some odd reason, I found Jimmy made better sense when I talked with him at night, in bed, under the covers, with only a night-light glowing.

During one of these late-night chats, I happened to start playing with a puppet that had been left out on the bed. I placed the puppet on my hand and started 'talking' to Jimmy through the puppet. I was amazed by my son's responses.

'What's your name?' I asked in a squeeky cartoon-type voice, and got the expected response. Jimmy had recently requested that everyone call him 'Jim', instead of Jimmy and began to lecture the puppet on his new-found preference. I asked the usual static questions about his family, and what he liked to do. Jimmy and I had a nice back-and-forth discussion about all the characters in the *Ghostbusters* movie. I was pleased with how well he was maintaining the conversation. I decided to push further to see what more I could learn.

'What's your teacher's name?' Jimmy correctly responded. My pulse quickened.

'Who are some of the kids in your class?' To my amazement, Jimmy began to rattle off some of the boy's names. Why would he be able to talk to the puppet, and not to me?

I continued the use of the puppet for many months during bedtime. Within a few weeks, I could get Jimmy to talk about his feelings, albeit in a limited way, about school and family issues. For some time, the puppet, who Jimmy called 'Frankie', was the only way I could learn what was going on inside my son's head – what his thoughts and feelings were. Jimmy would talk about his fears over the special school assembly that happened that week, or talk about the story in his school reading book. He also began talking about how he felt about his sister. The angry feelings he was experiencing were discussed and through the puppet I taught Jimmy about jealousy, and how it was a 'normal' feeling that many kids have. Gradually, Jimmy outgrew the puppet and began to feel comfortable just talking to me. I grew to love those late night conversations, and despite the guilt I had about not having quality time with my daughter, I was secretly happy that his sister was long asleep. She would not have understood why I was spending more time with her brother. It was as if Jimmy and I were trying to cram a whole day's worth of conversations into a 20-minute time frame.

'Tell me about heaven,' Jimmy asked me one night. We had been talking about his grandfather and what happens after we die.

'I don't remember anything about heaven. I know that it's a wonderful place, a happy place.'

'Is Pop there?'

'Yes, he is there, with Heavenly Father and Jesus.'

'Why did Heavenly Father send me here if heaven is my home?'

'I think that He sends us here to learn like at school. Then after we die, we go back home to live with Pop, and Jesus, and all of our family again.'

'Did I know you back in heaven?'

'I'm sure that you did. I'll bet that we made a deal together that we would help each other learn while we were here too.'

'So,' Jimmy said drowsily. 'You promised to help me learn what things mean in life, and I promised to help you learn what life means.' He shut his eyes. Sleep was creeping across his face. I was stunned. Did Jimmy really understand the profound meaning that came within the subtlety of what he just said?

'You're doing a good job of that son,' I said, tears beginning to well up in my eyes. 'I think we still have a long way to go, but we'll do it together, OK?'

'I love you Mommy.' Jimmy's last words of the day. His little body spent, arm outstretched, exhausted from the day's hurly-burly. This was perhaps the longest conversation I had ever had with my son, and the most meaningful of my life. It was one of those 'Mommy-Moments' that God gives us – the snippets in life that are burned into the fibers of our souls; the reserves that we draw upon to get us through life's next challenge.

9

Drugs?

I sat in the auditorium with about a thousand other parents. We were there to listen to one of America's most well known researchers on learning disability give us his thoughts on Attention Deficit Disorder. I was amazed at the sheer numbers of people who had all paid $45 to gather and listen to this man, and took comfort in knowing that I wasn't the only one who thought lunch came with the registration cost. Like me, each of the others had their own silent struggles with children who didn't quite fit into the mainstream. There were even some faces there that I recognized. We were all in the same boat, worrying about the children we loved. Wondering how we were going to help them learn what things mean in life.

The speaker was a tall, lanky man, with a rumpled coat and tie. His hair was a shock of brown that needed tidying in the worst way. He was a published author, had credentials out the kazoo, and was very respected by all. I had read some of his work and saw eye-to-eye on everything he said. Somehow, when seeing the man, my expectations of a polished professional flew out the window. I was amused. This guy could be a grown-up Jimmy – a totally witty, loveable, geek!

The lecture was very well done. Despite his bumbling Ichabod Crane appearance, the doctor had some very important things to say, all of which convinced me that ADD was the answer to my son's difficulties. Not only did he touch on the academic issues; he was the first professional I had ever heard to speak eloquently of the *social* difficulties, saying that kids with ADD are always the last ones to 'get the joke'. This statement really resonated with me, and I was convinced that I was on the right track. Despite the neurologist's examination and wavering opinions, my son *had* Attention Deficit Disorder. This was a concept that I could wrap my arms around, as opposed to the nebulous Central Auditory Processing Delay label the school gave Jimmy. Finally, there was published information that described my kid! In the two years I had been searching, I had never seen anything written that satisfied me.

The professional also talked about the annoying behaviors of kids with ADD, and how they have significant trouble making friends because their demeanor is so off-putting. This made perfect sense to me. Jimmy would stand and talk nonsense to someone about his movies, or videos, making everyone feel somewhat uncomfortable. When my friends would talk to Jimmy, I'd often get a searching look that silently spoke, 'How do I react to this? I don't understand a thing your son is trying to tell me.' Not everyone wanted to hear *ad nauseum* about how the trains ran on time on the Island of Sodor. If one of his classmates had seen one of the movies that Jimmy was fixated on, he stood half a chance of having a minimal conversation, providing Jimmy responded to the overtures at all. Otherwise, the teacher reported, his classmates had no clue what Jimmy was even trying to talk to them about. He was always thinking about something else. His comments were always tangential to what was actually going on around him. I could always see a relationship; you could figure out the multi-step logic process that Jimmy used, what he was saying made perfect sense. The problem was, most everyone couldn't. I had to follow my son around like a shadow, interpreting his vocal thoughts to all who came in contact with him.

I had convinced myself that ADD was the answer and after a great amount of research, I was sure that the drug Ritalin was worth looking into. I was all set to give things a try, but knew that I was going to have quite a challenge persuading my husband. Every decision he's made has been a long, torturous process and I knew that convincing him to give Ritalin a try would not be easy.

With the news of the ADD diagnosis, both Jim and I decided it was time to change pediatricians. We had attended a presentation given by a local pediatrician, whose specialty was caring for learning disabled children. We were both impressed enough to meet with him and ended up transferring our children's medical records to the new office. As much as we respected our previous doctor, we both felt that we needed to start a long-term relationship with a pediatrician who had experience prescribing medications such as Ritalin, and who was savvy in navigating the minefield of special education.

After several consultations with the new doctor, Jim still wasn't convinced that Jimmy should be placed on Ritalin. Chief among his concerns was possible addiction and the idea that his son would be taking a psychotropic medication. The drug was listed among the highest restricted by our government. I was very frustrated, and felt he was being very stubborn and unreceptive. I gathered research material that addressed his concerns, insisted he attend lectures, and scheduled appointments with our new pediatrician. On the advice of Deanie, I had done a trial of giving Jimmy a small glass of Coca-Cola in the morning with breakfast. The caffeine-laced drink seemed to perk him up and was an indicator that stimulant medication would be beneficial. Despite all this, Jim still wouldn't budge from his anti-medication position. Weeks had passed and I felt like Jimmy was going into a black hole, while his father stewed over the issues.

'I don't buy the idea that we have to give our son a stimulant to get him to settle down and concentrate,' said Jim. We were in what had to be our seventh round of heated talks on the subject.

'Didn't you read anything I gave you!' I railed, throwing my hands up in exasperation. 'Think about this,' I countered. 'When you were a little kid, sitting in church, and you knew that you had to be quiet or else the pastor and all the old ladies would shoot you dirty looks, how did you feel after it was all over and you could go home?'

'What are you getting at?'

'Did you feel like running around and climbing the trees, or did you just want to go up to your room and take it easy?'

'Well, I was kind of wiped out.'

'Exactly! Think of all the mental energy that it took to keep your little body quiet. You were pooped at the end of the service, right?'

'So what does this have to do with Jimmy?'

'It takes extra energy for Jimmy to pay attention to the things he needs to be concentrating on,' I said. 'Right now, for some reason, he doesn't have the energy in his brain that he needs to concentrate. So we help him by giving him a stimulant.'

'You mean we give our son drugs,' Jim said derisively.

'That's right, we give our son drugs,' I shot back. 'If our son had diabetes, would you withhold insulin? If he had high blood pressure, would you not allow him access to medication?'

'I still don't like the idea of our son on drugs.' Jim was worried that Jimmy would become addicted and would seek out drugs that were progressively stronger. He was also very resistive to the label 'drug dependent'.

'I want him to function without drugs.'

'So do I, but we can't ignore the problem here! Do you recall the doctor saying that many times these kids use the Ritalin as sort of a 'training wheel' to jump start the appropriate behaviors that they need to learn?' I was launching into my frontal assault. We were told that in many cases, the use of the drug is discontinued once the child has developed listening skills and increased their functioning through behavioral interventions.

Jim stalked off. I had overwhelmed him again. He went to the living room and assumed the supine position in the recliner chair, his hand grasped around the TV remote control in a death grip. His favorite TV show, *Star Trek* was coming on.

While Jim settled in to watch the 'final frontier', I threw on my coat and took a walk around the block to cool off. I heard William Shatner say, 'Beam me up, Scotty', just as the door slammed. I snorted in disgust, totally frustrated by the lack of progress I'd made convincing my husband that Jimmy needed to try the medication.

'Hmph! Beam *me* up too, Scotty,' I grumbled, kicking a small stone down the sidewalk. We were at a stalemate. Jimmy wasn't getting any better. Even if the drug didn't work, we owed him the chance of trying it. Why couldn't I get my husband to see this? I failed to understand what I perceived as a knee-jerk reaction on my husband's part to administering a controlled substance to our son.

Several weeks later, both Jim and I were on the phone with my parents. During our lengthy discussion about Jimmy's status, we fell into the topic of medication and the doctor's recommendation of Ritalin. To my surprise, Jim led the conversation, outlining all his concerns with my father, who at the time was the head athletic trainer for a large university. He was involved with all the athletes, many who competed at a world-class level, and was privy to their medical histories.

'I have quite a bit of experience with athletes who take Ritalin,' offered Dad. 'Many of them have been on it for years and couldn't function well without it. They're not addicted.'

Jim asked a few more questions, his mind clearly centered on the image of a raucous, hyperactive, football wide receiver on Ritalin, who never attends classes and can't make the grade.

'I don't think you need to worry,' my father reassured. 'The guys I'm talking about are Academic All-Americans. Some are married with kids. We're talking the cream of the crop. The percentage of athletes taking Ritalin for ADD is very high and they're all regular, normal guys. They study, learn the playbooks and get good grades. I wouldn't see anything dangerous about giving my grandson a trial of the medication. If anything, I would encourage it.'

We both rang off after the call and I was hopeful that Dad's words had gotten through to Jim. That evening, I would let the question lie. If I hoped to get any kind of response, I would have to wait for it. Pushing any further would only aggravate my husband.

The next day I got a call from Jim at the office. He'd had a good night's sleep, spent the morning's commute thinking about the whole question and had wanted to tell me that he could finally support the decision to try the medication. 'Call up the doctor and get the prescription.' My Dad had been the ally I needed in this battle to help Jim see my point of view. My fingers raced through my Rolodex for the doctor's number.

In America, there has been a cry that parents who put their kids on medication for ADD are taking the easy way out, abdicating their responsibilities as nurturers and disciplinarians. I found out first-hand that nothing could be further from the truth. The process of getting a prescription for a controlled substance, and then getting authorization to have a school nurse administer the drug to your child during the school day, is bureaucracy of paperwork. No parent would willingly wish this, or see medication as the 'easy way out'.

First I had to schedule an appointment with the doctor to obtain the prescription. In America, Ritalin, like most stimulants, is a 'Schedule II' drug and tightly controlled by law. This means that the only way to fill a prescription is to present the pharmacy with a written prescription – no phone-ins, faxes, or refills allowed. Also, the prescription must be filled within 72 hours of its being written, or the pharmacist won't fill it – a little-known rule that I learned about the hard way. Later, when I made my monthly 22-mile drive to the pediatrician's for additional prescriptions, I would have to take Jimmy to the doctor's office with me so the nurse could administer a monthly blood test called a CBC. This was required by law in the state we live in. Then I had to drive all the way back to the pharmacy and have the prescription filled, lest any delay put me over the 72-hour rule.

The school regulations were a whole different set of hoops to jump through: I had to fill out the school's required forms, which required the doctor's signature. After a back and forth between the doctor's office and the school, and the forms were in order, I had to personally drop off the medication to the nurse at her office. One time, I tried slipping the bottle in Jimmy's backpack in a sealed envelope with a note to the nurse. I immediately got a friendly call from the principal telling me I had done a 'No-No' and the rules said I had to come personally and make the monthly 'drug drops'. I went through this whole 'rigmarole' every month for two years. Sure – I was taking the easy way out.

Admittedly, I was a bit nervous the first day Jimmy took the medication. As much as I wanted this drug to be the end-all solution, the niggling thoughts in the back of my mind spoke to me as I was handing him the yellow pill. As Jimmy chewed the bitter pill, my mind wandered. *What if he turns into a werewolf or something?* I shook off the thoughts as lunacy, giggling to myself. My father-in law often endearingly referred to me as a 'flaky broad.' In this instance, I had to admit he was right.

I sent Jimmy to school on the bus and followed later in my car. I parked on the street and walked into the building, my hand clutched around the little bottle in my coat pocket that held my greatest hope. I felt as though I hacked away some of the vines that had been surrounding us, and could begin to see light at the end of this tunnel of fog and uncertainty we were traveling through. If the Ritalin wasn't the answer, I still felt as though I had made a giant step closer towards getting to the heart of the matter.

I walked into the nurse's office and introduced myself. I was nervous. What would she think? Was my kid the only one who was taking drugs? Since Jimmy's dose at lunchtime was 7.5 ml of Ritalin, I needed to cut several of the 5 ml pills in half. The nurse made a space for me at her desk and began searching for a spare bottle so we could divide the medication. As she opened her desk drawer, I saw a few dozen bottles of medication, each with a child's name on it. My heart soared. Jimmy would not be the only one reporting to the nurse's office at lunchtime. I wasn't the only mother jumping through bureaucratic hoops just to get medicine for my child at school.

The nurse always kept the door of her office open and I could catch a look at the pedestrian traffic in the halls. As I was getting ready to leave, I caught a fleeting glimpse of Debbie Dono passing the doorway as she was walking quickly towards the classrooms. She quickly backtracked and came into the nurse's office.

'Did you give Jimmy the medication this morning?' she asked excitedly. Her eyes were glistening, and my thought at that moment was a reflection of how much she cared about Jimmy's situation.

I nodded yes. 'I'm here on my first "drug run".' I joked.

'I have exciting news for you,' Debbie was just about stammering. 'Jimmy participated for the first time in speech today.'

I had never anticipated this. This was too good to be true. Both Debbie and I knew that it was impossible for a breakthrough to come this quick. It would take a few days for the drug to get into Jimmy's system. It had to be a coincidence. 'What did he do? What did he say?' I was thrilled, as was Debbie.

'We were talking about the holidays and how President's Day was coming up,' Debbie said. Her eyes were beginning to well up. If she went any further emotionally, I would break down and cry for joy right there in the nurse's office. I tried to maintain my composure as I listened to her. 'Jimmy told the group that George Washington's picture is on the dollar bill.'

I stood and looked at Debbie. We both knew the significance of the day's speech session for Jimmy. This was a breakthrough. For the first time, Jimmy had followed a conversation and made a contribution without being asked a question as a lead in. We were amazed and proud of Jimmy.

'I can't tell you how pleased I am,' she said, suddenly looking away. She was fighting her emotions too. It would have been unprofessional for us to start blubbering there in the nurse's office.

She excused herself on the premise that she wanted to share the news with the teachers. I said I had more errands to run.

As I started the engine of my car. I said a quick prayer in my heart, thanking God for Debbie and her hard work; I thanked Him for the wonders of pharmacology, even though I doubted that was the real reason for Jimmy's breakthrough – I just wanted to cover all my bases. Lastly, I asked Him to bless the genius whose idea it was to put George Washington's face on the one-dollar bill. We were one small step closer to getting our answers.

10

Out to Lunch

After a year on the Ritalin, Jimmy still had significant difficulties. The burst of language he had the day he first started the medication turned out to be a fluke. Both his teachers and I knew this was no garden-variety case of ADD. There was something more. We just couldn't put our finger on it. Second grade for Jimmy was a year in the twilight zone. Even though there was a new teacher, there was thankfully a good bit of continuity for Jimmy. Normally, special education classes such as Jimmy's are moved from school to school each year; squeezed in where the enrollments are low and extra classroom space is available. It was divine intervention that Jimmy was assigned the same school for the third year, an almost unheard of thing in our school district. Luckily for us, Debbie was still his speech teacher, Bernice Fajgier, a teacher's aide, remained with the class again this year, and a wonderful bus driver named Mary Lou was assigned our route for a second year in a row.

Academically, Jimmy seemed to be making progress the same rate as the other students. Where he seemed to be lacking was the social component. It was very perplexing for the teachers. It was as if the older Jimmy got, the more difficult it became for him to function in his environment. Every noise would distract him, he didn't seem to understand or have the capability to interact with the other students in his class, and the daily trip to the lunch room would turn him into a zombie.

'I just can't seem to get him to eat his lunch,' worried Mrs. Fajgier. 'It's not as though he is busy talking with the other kids, which is what I often have to scold the bunch about. Jimmy just sits there, staring off into space, sometimes with his hands over his ears.' Of course, we thought the culprit was the Ritalin, which was known to suppress appetite. I made sure Jimmy got a multi vitamin at home and ate a good supper. There was not much I could do about his food intake at school. Mrs. Fajgier wasn't going to force him to eat his lunch. She was too kind to do that. Blessedly, she watched over Jimmy like a mother hen.

Debbie would call me regularly with updates on the little breakthroughs that Jimmy would have in class. Around Christmas time that year, she called me all excited about Jimmy's new expressive language skills. 'Guess what Jimmy said today?' she asked.

'No telling,' I said, wondering if she was going to tell me another version of the King Arthur story. One day in class, Jimmy had fancied himself as King Arthur, and the rest of the students were the 'knights' all sitting around Debbie's 'Round Table'. Debbie could always count on Jimmy for a gem. When he spoke, Jimmy could never distinguish between fantasy and reality. We all knew he was pretending, but he didn't have the language skills to *say* he was pretending. I harbored secret visions of my son as an adult, getting hauled off to the hospital for the mentally insane because he walked around telling others he was 'King Arthur'.

'I asked Jimmy what he was thinking about today,' said Debbie. 'He told me that he was pretending to have x-ray vision!' It took me a minute to let it sink in why Debbie was so excited. 'Today was the first time Jimmy was able to verbally differentiate between the reality of other's perceptions and his pretend play, she said gleefully. 'He used the word PRETEND!' It took Debbie almost three years to get Jimmy to understand that it was important to say 'pretend' when talking about his daydreams.

This was also the year that Jimmy got his first taste of teasing by his peers. There was a new boy in the class who was what I would call a 'free spirit'. He would often spout the first thing that came off the top of his head. We all know some kids who thrive on being the agitator, and this kid was it. I was often in the class and grew to know this boy very well and could see that all his bluster was without malice. He was just one of those kids who bumped into all of life's experiences with both arms outstretched. From Jimmy's perspective, he was loud, unpredictable and was like sand in his shoe. One minute, the two were best buddies, the next minute, Jimmy would be churning inside because of some innocent teasing.

One day, Jimmy came home angry. 'I'm not an idiot!' he seethed. This was a first for me. I rarely got to see any emotion out of my son. I was actually pleased. I correctly guessed who the name-caller was.

'When did he call you an idiot?'

'Outside.'

'What did you do?'

Silence, which was probably what happened on the school playground that day.

'Did he call some of the other kids idiots too?'

Jimmy rattled off a few names of some of the boys. I was pleased that he had the names on the tip of his tongue!

'Well then, it sounds to me like he calls everybody an idiot. Sometimes kids and even grownups say things that aren't really true. Remember how Mommy yells at the other drivers when she's driving the car? I call them idiots.'

Jimmy looked at me. I could see the cogs working. Something was starting to sink in. I wanted him to understand that he didn't have to take everything so personally. The whole thing mystified me. Why can most kids get into a verbal sparring match, and seem to laugh it off? My little boy gets called an idiot, and takes it literally! Why is everything so black and white with him?!

One time we went to a public park while on vacation. There was a noisy group of children playing, some boys Jimmy's age. Caroline immediately joined the fun game of chase and tag. Jimmy stood high up on the top of the slide, away from the rumble below. One of his favorite movies at the time was *The Rocketeer*. He fancied himself as being able to fly with a rocket strapped to his back. Since the characters in the movie chewed Beemans chewing gum, Jimmy had me crazily searching all over the stores for the hard to find brand. I stood and observed, hoping he wouldn't take a flying dive off the top of the sliding board. As I watched, I noticed that it was as though Jimmy wanted to engage the other children, but didn't quite know what to do. They were loud, unpredictable, unknown – total strangers.

'Hey! Let's get him!' shouted one of the older boys, looking up at Jimmy. The group climbed up the ladder and surrounded Jimmy, who froze. The kids' only intention was to include Jimmy in their game. Jimmy didn't understand that. He couldn't 'read' the social situation. From the horror exhibited on his face, the wild bunch was coming up the ladder to 'get him,' or in his hard-core literal-interpretative mind they meant to 'kill him' or at the very least, beat him to a pulp. He totally shut down inside and blanked out. A melt-down in reverse.

Part of me wanted to intervene and take Jimmy down off the top of the slide like a lost kitten out of a tree. But he was a seven-year-old. Against my better judgement, I let the situation develop to see if Jimmy could find a way to deal with this social dilemma. It would have been worse socially, in my mind, for his Mama to bail him out. I watched as things unraveled.

'C'mon!' said the largest boy. 'Don't you want to play?' By this time a group of four had surrounded Jimmy, who had the look of a trapped mouse. He put his hands over his ears and cowered. It wasn't hard for the boys to smell fear. Jimmy was physically bigger than all of the boys.

'What's the matter with you?!' one crowed sarcastically. 'Are you a retard or something?'

As soon as I heard the 'retard' word, I could no longer let it go. I had to intervene. 'Jimmy,' I said with the most authoritarian voice I could muster, with my heart breaking inside. This was the first time I had ever fully witnessed my son being teased. 'Tell the boys that you do not want to play.' Four pairs of eyes first fell to me, then trailed off to see if their own parents were within earshot.

'Jim!' I emphasized. 'Tell the boys that you do not want to play.' Everyone stood and waited for Jimmy. I waited to give him time to respond. The boys paused for their own entertainment, wanting to see what this kid would do. I was dying inside. My son was not a freak show!

'Tell the boys that you do not want to play.' I said as calmly and succinctly as I could, the tears trying to brim up to my eyes.

'I'm not a retard!' Jimmy mumbled, his hands still over his ears, he was crouched with his knees under his chin, rocking to and fro. The boys looked at each other with that triumphant, knowing look. The nonverbal communication was unmistakable. 'Too bad the mother was around, or we would have had a jolly good time teasing this one.'

'Jimmy,' I said again. 'You need to tell the boys that you do not want to play. The boys do not know that you don't want to play. You need to tell them before you come down.' I wanted to drive home the point on two levels. The boys needed to know that their 'mark' had troubles of his own and shame, shame, on them for their teasing. On the other hand, I felt it was important to give Jimmy a real-life lesson in social skills. If this kind of scenario ever popped up again, perhaps Jimmy might recall the phrase; 'I don't want to play.'

Jimmy suddenly slid down the sliding board. He walked over to me, turned to the boys and said loudly, 'I don't want to play.'

I gave Caroline 'the look' that signified that it was time to leave. She stalked off, shot the boys a disgusted look and shouted, 'He just doesn't like to play with other kids. You should have just left him alone.' Clearly her fun was ruined by the incident. I felt bad that she had to be socially impacted in such a negative way. She would have had a fun time playing with the other children. But now, the family was walking away, because of her brother's difficulties fitting in. 'I'm not a retard,' said Jimmy as we left the park. Just as he perseverated over the 'idiot' episode earlier that year, Jimmy would talk about this incident for months.

At the end of his third year in school, Jimmy's eligibility for continued special education services came up for review. This involved testing by psychologists, evaluations by speech pathologists, and an interview with the social worker. Even though I knew in my heart that he would remain in the program, the little spurts of doubt crept in. I felt Jimmy's placement in the Communication Handicapped program was totally appropriate. Silly as it may seem, I kept asking myself, 'What if?' The questions were hard to shake off and preoccupied my mind for several weeks.

I was a bit nervous when the day came for my interview with the school social worker. The meeting started out with the usual list of questions. How was the medication working? How did I feel about his school placement? We talked about life at home. I ran down the list of his chores and responsibilities, talked about how much Jimmy liked to read late into the night and how I often found books in his bedcovers the next morning, discussed his self-esteem, which I thought was intact. 'He seems like a kid who is comfortable with who he is,' I said. As nervous as I was, I tried to give her a complete and thorough picture of who my son is.

'He loves to eat fruit,' I said, recounting how I was amused that his class all knew that Jimmy's favorite food was grapes. I told her how Jimmy loved to play his Sonic the Hedgehog video games and how he dealt with the frustration of not advancing through a certain spot in the game by throwing the hand control aside and stalking off to his room with that dark look on his face. We commented on how his favourite color was green. I told her how I would often take Jimmy out with me on writing assignments for my weekly newspaper column. It was on one of these jaunts where Jimmy developed an appreciation for the Civil War era and started asking questions about his genealogy. The psychologist was a regular reader of my column and commented how I quoted the children at times, yet did not emphasize that Jimmy was a 'special child'. I also mentioned to her that Jimmy had received his Bobcat badge in the Cub Scouting program earlier that month. Jimmy's favourite book at the time was *The Legend of Sleepy Hollow*, and we both chuckled at Jimmy's need to recite the whole story verbatim, whilst assuming the 'Caesar Pose.' She told me she thought him to be a very likeable and charming young man. I felt as though I was rambling on and on.

After about 20 minutes, the social worker closed her folder. 'You know, Mrs. Fling,' she said. 'It is a pure pleasure working with you.'

I was surprised. This was not the finger wagging that I was half-expecting.

'I have never worked with a parent who knows their child as well as you do,' she said. 'I work with many parents who don't have any idea, much less care about their children's favourite video games, learning style, or state of mind. I hope you don't mind my saying that it is refreshing as a professional to work with a parent like you.'

I was stunned. My face began to feel warm. 'You know, I honestly walked in here today thinking that I wouldn't measure up.'

We both laughed. 'Your comments mean a great deal to me,' I said. 'As you know, the position of mother doesn't often get an on-the-job performance review from a professional. Who do I ask for a raise?'

All kidding aside, I thanked the social worker for her kind words. I went out to the car, took six deep breaths, drove home and called my mother and thanked her for doing a good job of raising Jimmy's mother. We both cried on the phone, in part because we both know that praise does not come often enough for mothers who work to shape the future of the world's children. We appreciated the significance of the social worker's praise, it would prove to be a reserve to draw from when the doubts about my effectiveness as a parent would come.

The third grade is a year where the rubber hits the road. For all nine-year-old children in the United States, it is a time when increased demands are made of them both socially and academically, and most parents hear the moaning of their children who pine for the days when 'things were easier'. This was a year that we nearly lost Jimmy.

Providence was on our side again this year. We had a new classroom teacher. Miss C. was fresh out of school, had a newly minted degree in special education and this was her first class. At first I wasn't too thrilled by her lack of experience, but a friend of mine, who knew the inner workings of district politics, calmed my fears. 'I saw her during her student teaching and she's very good,' she said. 'You have nothing to fear. She has a real good handle on communication-based teaching.' She was right. God had again blessed us with a very good teacher.

Adding to our fortune was the re-assignment of Debbie as the speech teacher, Mrs. Fajgier as the classroom assistant, and Mary Lou, the bus driver with a heart of gold who always gave Jimmy a high-fiver at the end of the day's run.

Debbie kept in regular contact with me, providing anecdotes of the wonderfully unusual way that Jimmy looks at life. One day she told me that she had introduced the group to a unit on letter writing. All the students would write a letter to a famous celebrity and hope that they would get a letter in return.

'But Mrs. Dono,' Jimmy said. 'We already know how to write our A B Cs!' Debbie stopped dead in her tracks, trying to figure out where Jimmy was coming from. With a giggle, she quickly realized that here was yet another case of 'literal interpretation' from Jimmy who thought it was a dumb idea to write the A B Cs to somebody

famous like Steven Spielberg. Debbie had to explain the difference
between 'writing a letter' and 'writing letters'. Jimmy chose to write
to the Hollywood director, asking him 'if he got to ride in a
limousine', and some weeks later he received a nice form letter and
autographed photo. It meant the world to him.

In the classroom, Jimmy had a rough go from the very
beginning of that year. His teacher reported that he often appeared
overwhelmed and fearful, easily agitated. Little behaviors that
formerly slipped by unnoticed suddenly grew more intense. It
seemed as though everything about Jimmy became more intense as
more demands were being placed on him. His teacher, the aide and
everyone on the team began to worry about him. Although he was
making quantum leaps in academic areas and in some of his
language, it seemed as though his difficulties were becoming more
pronounced. Jimmy was starting to *look* handicapped.

Things that were happening at school started to creep into
more areas at home. Jimmy was becoming more and more
withdrawn. It was as though I was losing him to some internal
stimulation that held more of an appeal to him. He began to hum
more loudly at home and at school. He would often mutter to
himself, many times gesticulating with his hands. Months later, I
would catch him sitting for minutes at a time, just waving his hands
in front of his face, deeply engrossed in acting out a video he'd seen.

I took more time to simply observe my son and I became
frightened by what I saw. One morning, I watched from the dining
room window as he waited for the bus in front of the driveway. He
had recently managed to get over his sheer terror of going outside
the house. But his eyes were constantly roving the street for any
stray dog or cat that happened by. I looked on as Jimmy paced back
and forth, across the end of the driveway. His mind was clearly on
something, his hands were flapping, and he was talking to himself.
Anyone observing him must surely think he was acting like one of
those dotty homeless types who are so commonly seen in the large
cities.

That was it! Yes! He looked just like one of those crazy homeless people! The realization of the cognitive comparison sickened me. What kind of future is my son to have? My impression of the homeless is that they find themselves in dire situations only after a life of harrowing misfortunes. Yet, here, my son's life was just beginning!

The episodes carried over into school. His teacher reported her concern that he was very antisocial and suggested that I surreptitiously observe Jimmy during the lunch-time recess. One sunny day, I drove over to the school, parked my car down the street, and watched as the kids came out to the play yard after lunch. What I saw only added to the bleak picture I had observed earlier in front of the house. After the class had come out, the children immediately began playing a game with a ball. Mrs. Fajgier tried several times to redirect Jimmy towards the fun. One or two of the other children came over to talk to Jimmy during the course of the free period. These attempts had no impact on my son. He simply was too involved in his mind's inner thoughts to give much attention to the other children and their game.

'Don't give up!' I silently exhorted the other children. 'Keep trying to get his attention.' After fifteen minutes, it was clear that Jimmy would not be drawn out. I sat in my parked car in tears. My son was somewhere else in his mind, pacing like a homeless man, waving his arms and ranting to himself about who knows what. How could I help him when he appeared to withdraw so deeply into his own shell?

I was at my wit's end. This was so disturbing to me. Clearly Jimmy's troubles were not ADD. It was something more. Much, much, more. Sadly, I had to admit to myself that we needed to see another specialist. After I had resolved to go another round with the doctors, my husband came home with some disturbing news. His company was changing their health insurance system. We would no longer be able to afford the premiums for the care we had been accustomed to. We could no longer choose our own doctors and specialists. Through sheer economics, his company was forcing all employees to use the doctors who were members of a Health Maintenance Organization, or HMO. This is a health care company that contracts with an employer to provide, or administer, health care services to employees. The employee must chose a health care provider from the specified network of professionals for their medical care. If they go out of the network, they must pay full price.

I was seething. I had spent years carefully finding the right people to take care of Jimmy's special needs and now my husband's company was going to dictate which doctors I can now use! When the word came out what company was administering the HMO, I quickly learned that not a single doctor we used was part of the approved network! If we continued to go to them, it would now cost us full price.

Call me spoiled rotten, but I cried for two days straight over the matter. I was in a murderous rage. Didn't those administrative cost-cutters know that you don't mess with a mother of a handicapped child when it comes to her medical care providers? After the third day, I realized there was nothing I could do about it. I never felt so helpless in all my life. Jim had done an inquiry about the costs of remaining on our present program and the monthly premiums amounted to 50 per cent of our net take-home pay. I was despondent. Every single one of our doctors was being taken away from us. We could no longer afford to use them. I had to go back to square one and start searching all over.

About a month after the medical insurance changeover, I got a phone call from the school psychologist. She wanted to discuss an 'incident' involving Jimmy at school. My spirits sank. What was it now?

'We felt it was important to let you know what has happened,' she began. I braced myself for the worst. 'The other day, when the class was preparing to go to lunch, Jimmy was selected to be the line leader,' she began.

'What was the problem?' I asked patiently, wondering how this could translate into an 'incident'.

'Jimmy's job was to lead the class down the hall to the lunchroom,' continued the psychologist. 'The class followed as Jimmy led them right into the music room. They all thought it was funny Mrs. Fling, but when the teachers went in to see why they all went in there, the class was all giggling, thinking Jimmy had played a joke, but when they looked at Jimmy, he seemed disoriented and confused.'

I saw the ramifications of what she was trying to tell me. After four years at the school, with the lunchroom in direct sight of the classroom, my son had failed to be able to find his way from his classroom to the lunchroom – a trip he's taken everyday he's attended the school. The teachers and psychologist both encouraged me to take Jimmy to the doctors for another round of tests.

'Do you know that my husband's company just threw us into an HMO?' I asked. 'I don't have any confidence in their ability to take care of this. It'll be a huge fight just to get the necessary permission to see any specialists. Can't the school do anything to help?'

'Do what you can from your end first,' said the psychologist. 'Then we'll take it from there if need be.'

I felt as though my insides had been ripped apart. The only option was to go begging the new HMO. I had never begged for anything in my life. If my son was to have any hope, I would have to stuff all my pride in my pocketbook, walk into the doctor's office and be as persuasive as possible. Jimmy's future depended on it.

Up to this point in my life, intense, soul-searching prayer had never been a big part of my day-to-day living. Things had always gone so easily for me that I had not really needed to fall on my knees in total humility and ask for help from a higher source. Prayer always came easily and frequently as I thanked God for my blessings. It was the 'asking' part that I had trouble with. I had been taught the importance of prayer from the time I was a very young child. With a little bit of shame, I have to admit that this kind of prayer has always been a difficult thing for me. I have never been able to put my finger on the reason for this void. As a youngster, I had always been very shy. Perhaps it was the whole 'begging' aspect of prayer. Sometimes when I prayed, I got the sense that my words ended at the ceiling of my bedroom. As I grew older, another thought I had was perhaps there was a lack of humility on my part for me to get down on my knees and let it all hang out.

As a mother looking out for the best interests of a child, any pride I had was the first thing to go. I had always taken on the responsibility to learn everything there was about my son's condition and to work from there. But as I approached my fifth year without getting any answers, I was getting near the point of desperation. I fell onto my knees and poured my heart out in prayer. In my talk with God, I outlined all the things I knew, all the things I had studied, and all the things I needed to know in order to help my son. With tears of frustration coursing down my face, I pleaded with my Father in Heaven to be led to a place, a book – anything – where I could find the answers I needed to best help Jimmy. As I closed my prayer that night and let out a long sigh, almost immediately afterward I began to feel a warm comforting sensation deep within me. I was reassured that God had heard my prayer and understood the pain and frustration that this mother was feeling. I knew in my soul that soon I would find the answers that I needed. All I had to do was be patient, continue to listen to my heart, and keep knocking on doctors' doors.

11

Light at the End of the Tunnel

With my frustration level at an all-time high, I called and scheduled an appointment with our new primary care physician. Would I find answers with this new doctor? Or simply more confusion? Jimmy was nearly ten years old now. None of the labels the doctors, psychologists and education professionals had given us up to that point included all the problematic behaviors that Jimmy had. The auditory processing disability only addressed Jimmy's problems with language. The ADD label only concerned the attention problems. What about the rest of the issues? Wasn't there a definitive diagnosis out there that encompassed *all* the areas where Jimmy was experiencing difficulties? What about the obsessions, the rigidity, the constant anxiousness, the getting lost in his own school, the lack of friends?

On the day of Jimmy's appointment with the new doctor, I reluctantly told him where we were going only a few hours before the scheduled arrival time. Over the course of the last two years, Jimmy had become increasingly fearful and agitated when he had to go to the doctor's office. He would lose sleep, and fret obsessively over what was going to happen. I had learned that it was just better to give him information about upcoming appointments on a need-to-know basis. I could never figure out the reason for this behavior. Only years later did I learn from Jimmy that the reason he becomes so agitated with doctor visits is because of his extreme fear of the unknown. Jimmy is a boy who needs to know *exactly* what is going to happen in any given situation. I just didn't know how great a need this was at the time. When he found out about the appointment with the new doctor, his reaction was exactly what I expected. Jimmy immediately became very agitated. His skin first became mottled, he started hyperventilating and then he dissolved into tears. 'But Mom, I'm not sick! I don't need to go to see Dr. A.'

I caught myself short. He was not going to see his regular doctor. This new doctor would be a stranger. My stomach sank. 'You are not going to see Dr. A. today,' I said. 'We have a new doctor now. We are going to meet her and she will give you a regular check-up.'

Jimmy disappeared into his room. I gave him the space to digest the news. Meanwhile, I still had to make sure Caroline got out the door and to her school on time. I made myself busy packing her books and papers, getting her lunch pail ready, and straightening her pony tail. I hurried her through the before-school preparations because I knew the ritual of questions would soon come from Jimmy.

'What is going to happen at the doctor's office?' Jimmy sobbed. His face now a lovely shade of pastel green, reminiscent of bleached out surgical scrubs. He was on the verge of bringing up his breakfast. There was a look of terror in his eyes.

I ran down the list of things that I anticipated at the doctor's office, in as calm a voice as I could muster. I chatted about the wait in the waiting room, the check-in with the nurse, measuring height and weight, blood pressure, writing down the numbers in the charts. I gave Jimmy as much detail as I could. He seemed to be somewhat comforted in the past when I gave him as much detail as possible. I then told Jimmy the details of a physical exam, running over the drill with the tongue depressor, the stethoscope, and a look in the ears with the little thing with the light on it.

'Will the doctor bang my knees?' asked Jimmy.

'Yes, she will take her little rubber hammer and gently tap your knees and elbows to get your reflexes,' I said, gently tapping Jimmy's knees with my forefinger.

'Will I get a shot?' Jimmy asked with tears streaming down his face. He rarely cried, or showed any emotion at all. The sight of my son in such emotional distress was very unsettling to me. As much as I tried, I failed to understand the underlying reason for his panic at the thought of going to the doctor's office. In the past, I wanted to yell at him, 'Just be a big boy and stop crying.' The only thing that seemed to work to calm Jimmy was for me to present a calm voice and be very matter of fact about the visit, and do my best to remain patient when he asked over and over again for the rundown on the details.

'I promise that there will be no shot.'

Jimmy plunked his head down on his pillow. I went to look for my coat and car keys. I would go over the details four times in the car and six times in the waiting room before the nurse would call Jimmy's name.

After a 45-minute wait, we got back into the examining room area. 'What's wrong with Jimmy today,' said the nurse, looking down at my son, who was now in the throes of a full-blown panic. I was physically helping him through the hallway towards examining room three.

'Oh, we're just here to meet the doctor and to get a physical,' I said breezily for Jimmy's benefit. The nurse looked at me quizzically. I shot her back a look that spoke, 'Don't even ask!' We went through the motions of the height and weight. She attempted to place a blood pressure cuff on Jimmy but he balked. I suggested that perhaps the doctor could do that later as Jimmy got more comfortable.

The nurse took my son's chart and left, closing the door to the examining room. My son was visibly relieved. He sat on my lap and we went over the details again until we heard a short quick knock and the doctor walked in. I felt Jimmy stiffen in my arms. His breathing quickened, his face went green again. I quickly scanned the room for the location of the nearest rubbish pail in case he started vomiting.

'Hi! I'm Dr. R.,' said the young woman, holding her hand outstretched. Jimmy took it limply and shook it, refusing to look up at the doctor. We went through the perfunctory how-do-you-do's, and then she got down to the business of the physical exam. As Jimmy sat in my lap, the blood pressure was taken. Jimmy was invited to sit on the examining table but he refused to budge. All along, as the doctor moved to reflexes, and then listened with her stethoscope, I verbally spoke to Jimmy, reinforcing the details list that we had gone over so many times before. I don't know why I did this. It was instinctive.

Again, the doctor invited Jimmy to hop up on the examining table, asking him to take off his clothes so she could complete the rest of the exam. With every ounce of courage, Jimmy climbed down off my lap and walked toward the table. As the doctor reached to help my nine-year-old, he changed his mind and fell to the floor in a silent heap.

'I think we'll defer the rest of the exam until later,' said the doctor quietly, looking sadly at my son who was lying at our feet in a fetal position. 'This is clearly very traumatizing for him.'

As my son lay still on the floor, hands over his ears, the doctor and I discussed the issues. I wanted a referral to see specialists. Considering the fact that my son had just fallen apart emotionally before our eyes, I was confident that she would have no reason to withhold the precious referral paperwork. She scribbled 'Pervasive Developmental Disorder??' in Jimmy's chart. I had never heard the term before and made a mental note to follow-up on the term but it quickly left my thoughts. I had bigger questions on my mind, like how I was going to get my son back into the car, and whether I would get the required insurance papers. After another 20 agonizing minutes, I left with a referral to an audiologist, who would test Jimmy's hearing in hopes that we could find out why he was so sensitive to noise. We also got a referral to another pediatric neurologist affiliated with a highly-regarded children's hospital in nearby Philadelphia. I had just signed us up for two more rides on the medical merry-go-round, but this time, I felt we were close to finally finding the answer. I could feel it.

I scheduled the appointment with the audiologist and wrote the date on the family's kitchen calendar. My son, who I always thought was oblivious to matters of the home, had suddenly started screening the family calendar for doctor and dental visits.

'What's this?' he asked, tapping his finger on the kitchen calendar several days before the scheduled visit with the audiologist. I told Jimmy about the visit to the 'ear doctor'. I could not lie to my son, even if it meant that I had to endure the week of ritualistic querying about exactly what was going to happen at the doctor's office. I steeled myself in anticipation of being asked the same questions, over, and over again.

We arrived at the office of the 'ear doctor' for our morning appointment. The signage on the door indicated that this doctor's specialty was pediatric audiology. I knew within 90 seconds after checking-in that the comfort of children was not a priority at this office. The decor in the waiting room was austere, there were no magazines or toys to be seen and the staff was all dressed very formally. After taking in the scene, Jimmy proceeded to turn his usual green pallor, his anxiety level shot through the roof and for the fiftieth time, I went through the ritual of verbally laying out exactly what would happen, including the reassurance that there would be no shots. After 20 minutes of waiting, Jimmy was lying on the floor of the waiting area in the fetal position. I ignored the stares of the other patients as I gently reassured him.

After the routine question and answer preliminaries by the nurse, Jimmy and I sat and waited in the examining room for the doctor. Jimmy again insisted on sitting in my lap. I endured another 20-minute wait, my legs going numb from my nine-year-old's weight.

When the doctor entered the room, Jimmy stiffened. When I looked up to greet the man, it was all I could do to stifle a laugh. The character who came to examine my son was straight from central casting. His whole appearance screamed, 'medical doctor'. His stiffly starched white lab coat had his name stitched in bold blue letters, and the piece de resistance was the silver band around his head with a large round reflector. I thought Jimmy was going to jump out of his skin. After testing, the doctor told me that Jimmy's hearing was normal with no hypersensitivity to sound. Discouraged and doubtful that Jimmy had gotten the right kind of testing, I left the office, exhausted but bemused at the story I would later tell my husband about the pediatric specialist whose first impression was enough to scare the daylights out of any kid.

Several weeks later, Jimmy and I would drive into the city to meet with a pediatric neurologist. By this time my spirits were pretty low and I was burned out with the revolving door of doctors we'd seen over the years. In my mind, this trip would be my last. I would let it all hang out on this visit, whether the doctor had time for me or not. This poor doctor would hear every detail of life with Jimmy because I had learned with the previous neurologist, when I hadn't given the doctors all the information, they came up with an inconclusive diagnosis. This time, I planned on grabbing this guy by both lapels of his white lab coat and giving him a brain dump of information on my son. I had nothing to lose.

In the days leading up to the appointment, I made lists. I wanted to include everything that was worrisome about Jimmy's behaviors. This doctor was going to get as complete a picture as I could provide on my son in the average of four minutes that parents were allotted for such discourse during screening visits.

Of biggest concern was Jimmy's lack of social functioning. On this list, I wrote, 'no friends', 'doesn't understand how to talk to other kids but will talk the ear off of a grownup'. I had never brought this concern as a chief worry to any doctor before, largely because I didn't want to appear as a whiney mother: 'Nobody will play with my Jimmy!' For some odd reason, my inner voice said that this needed to be discussed.

Then I made the list of things that drove me nuts. Jimmy's interest in anything on TV or videos, how he used dialog to communicate, although things had improved a great deal with Debbie's intervention in speech class. However, he still obsessed about all the characters in the videos. I recently had to go outside and fetch Jimmy because he was tromping around the neighborhood with a beige trench coat on, magnifying glass in one hand, notepad and paper in the other. He was imitating the lead character in the recently released *Harriet the Spy* movie. The problem was that he wasn't as subtle at hiding behind the bushes and peeking at the neighbors as the lead character in the movie. Our neighbors had hired some help in to re-roof their house and the workman eyed Jimmy with amused suspicion as he watched my son go through exaggerated motions of stealthy spying. I was embarrassed as I hauled Jimmy back into the house by the collar of his Sunday-go-to-church trench coat.

Another topic on my list was how often life often had to stop if Jimmy's latest obsession wasn't satisfied. Again, as before, I was reluctant to openly discuss this area with a professional for fear they would say that I was just an overindulgent parent. My child's obsession with his videos is a hard thing to put into words. At best, I come off like a mother who is just spoiling a child. It is so hard to describe the *intensity* of his passion for the videos. 'So? My kid likes *Thomas the Tank Engine* too,' said one patronizing parent. If I let on that I had to shop in three states to find Benny and Bill toys, I risked sounding like a fool. Nobody understood.

Then there was Jimmy's strict adherence to things. He would go bonkers if I used bed sheets that were any color other than the royal blue he was used to. I made a lengthy list; 'tell doctor about the time he went bananas when I rearranged furniture in living room,' and 'won't wear any other clothes besides fleece pants and certain kinds of socks.' Other items on the list were Jimmy's frequent head banging, hand-flapping, humming, talking to himself, and general anxiety towards anything new, or if there was a change. I even made a note to tell him when Jimmy was a baby, he used to fall asleep every time he chewed on his peanut butter and jelly sandwich. He'd just conk right out. I'd have to open his mouth with my fingers and extract the gooey mess inside his mouth. Every behavior might serve to be a clue to a diagnosis that made sense!

Armed with my big list, and a map to Philadelphia, I loaded Jimmy in the car for the hour ride to the hospital. The closer we came the more agitated he got. As we approached the Walt Whitman Bridge and could see the city skyline, Jimmy grew violent and began pounding the window of the passenger side door. His face was that unmistakable shade of green. I prayed silently all the while, going through the verbal ritual of assuring him what was going to happen at the new doctor's office. As we drove across the bridge, Jimmy suddenly unfastened his safety belt and slumped down to the floor of the car, moaning. I thought he was going to vomit right there – mid-span. By the grace of God, I found my way to the parking garage without any wrong turns through the morning rush-hour traffic. After switching off the car's engine, I did some heavy Lamaze-type breathing. Next to me, on the floor, Jimmy was doing a little coping of his own. Both of us were emotionally exhausted and we hadn't even walked into the building yet!

After a relatively short wait, the staff called Jimmy into the examining room. He was very agitated and did not want to go at first, but I managed to coax him into it. To my pleasure, he stayed alone with the doctor for 20 minutes. Then the doctor called both of us in so he could chat with me. Jimmy refused to stay. 'It scares me when I hear you talk about me to the doctor,' he said. 'I want to wait in the waiting room.'

In a small way, it was a good thing that there was no distraction by Jimmy during my chat with the doctor, who I related my list of concerns with the intensity of a fire hose. He jotted in his notes furiously. Then he asked about Jimmy's language functioning and cognitive development. He was particularly concerned whether

Jimmy had a delay in his speech. 'Jimmy has always been able to speak clearly,' I said. 'It's just that sometimes we have had a tough time making the connection with what he's trying to tell us.' Then I reiterated that Jimmy knew his ABCs before he was one and was 'reading' books before age two. 'No cognitive problems there,' I said hopefully. 'People were telling us he was a genius when he was little, but now he is in special education. It just doesn't make sense.'

After several minutes, the doctor left, saying he wanted to consult some of his medical books. My mind wandered during the wait. I went out to take a peek in the waiting area. Jimmy was fine. His anxiety seemed to be under control as long as he didn't have to deal with the doctor directly. After what seemed like a five-minute wait, the doctor returned. He was clutching a well-worn, dog-eared copy of a red paperback book. The cover said, *DSM-IV.*

12

The Heart of My Artichoke

'Has anyone ever suggested Asperger Syndrome as a diagnosis for Jimmy?' asked the doctor.

'Gesundheit?' I said jokingly. 'How do you spell Asperger?' I had brought my notepad and had switched my brain into professional mode. The words, 'this is the heart of your artichoke,' kept flashing through my mind. 'Better take good notes.'

'I think Jimmy fits the criteria for Asperger Syndrome, which is an autistic spectrum disorder,' said the doctor. 'I had originally considered Pervasive Developmental Disorder (PDD-NOS), but was reluctant to diagnose this because of his language preservation. I think Asperger is a better fit because of Jimmy's interests in videos.'

My mind was swimming. Whoa! Whoa! Wait a minute! Autism! My skin crawled. This is not the kind of news I wanted to hear! The answer to my prayers was autism? And what did Jimmy's obsession with videos have to do with a diagnosis?

'You need to slow down a little bit here,' I said shakily to the doctor. 'You've given me a lot to process.' Fragments of what he was saying kept filtering in. I wrote in my notepad feverishly. 'Pervasive Developmental Disorder – close but not as good a fit as "Asparagus".' The word autism stopped my heart. It just didn't make sense. All I knew about autism was limited to a newspaper story I wrote several years ago about autistic kids competing in the Special Olympics. Those kids were very withdrawn, had difficulties with language, and were very resistant to change.... Then the magnitude of all the puzzle pieces began to hit me: my description of those autistic Olympians paralleled my own son, only on a vastly different level. Jimmy was resistant to change, he was very withdrawn with his peers, and he had difficulty with his pragmatic language. As my husband would say, 'same church – different pew.'

As the doctor continued to talk with me, I remembered the shiver that ran down my back. The word autism was so cold. I tried to listen but felt chilled to the bone. 'Lemme see that book you've got,' I said, reaching for his copy of the *Diagnostic and Statistical Manual of Mental Disorders – Fourth Edition*. I quickly glanced down Asperger Disorder's five diagnostic criteria categories, A through F:

It was all there! Impairment in social functioning; obsessive interests and rigidity; ability to use language to communicate, yet poor social and pragmatic skills; intact cognitive and self-help skills; repetitive motor mannerisms; and no peer relationships. I was astounded!

'I don't understand how you can say my son is autistic,' I said in frustration. 'He is a smart boy, who can talk...' In my mind, I wondered if this Asperger Syndrome was another fad diagnosis, or what we called in the news business the 'syndrome du jour'.

'There are different levels of autistic functioning,' said the doctor. 'There are the kids that you see who are totally withdrawn from the world around them, then we see individuals who are like the Dustin Hoffman character in *Rainman*, then there are very high functioning kids like Jimmy.'

'But what can we do about this?' I asked. 'Is there medication, a special program...?' The doctor was hesitant, saying there was no cure for this disorder. My heart sank. The treatment would be the same as with autistic individuals – training and coping programs. He suggested that I take Jimmy for a second opinion at another specialist, who could help with a program. I jotted down the new doctor's name and phone number. Then I wrote all the information down for the little diagnosis code book the doctor had, including the ISBN and page number for Asperger Disorder. My 20 minutes was up. I thanked the doctor, stuck my notepad in my purse and left the hospital knowing our life had just changed. It had been eight weeks to the day, since my prayerful epiphany.

As I drove home in silence, emotionally spent, I thought about how all the concerns I had about my son were listed as number code 299.80 of the *DSM-IV.* The rigid routines, the obsession with videos, ritualistic behaviors, speech and language difficulties, the stiff posture and funny facial gazes, and finally, it explained Jimmy's lack of friends.

I accepted the diagnosis with a mixture of emotion. On one hand, it was the happiest day of my life. I finally had an answer that made sense! At last I had a name for it! All the little things that had been bothering me were now part of the whole package – in one diagnosis. My five-year journey for an answer had finally come to an end. After years of peeling back thorny leaves, I finally had the heart of my artichoke!

After dinner that evening I sat down and went over my notes with Jim. He shared my mix of melancholy. While he was confident that the doctor had given us the answer we had looked for, his pleasure was tinged with the sadness of the permanency of Jimmy's condition. The doctor said there was no cure for Asperger Syndrome, just teaching and coping. The first place we turned for information was the Internet. Jim was much more skilled at doing web searches than I. The extent of my experience was sending off an e-mail here and there. Jim typed in 'Asperger' and a link came up for the OASIS website, which was created by Barb Kirby, the mother of a son with Asperger Syndrome. There, we found a paper called 'Asperger Syndrome Throughout the Lifespan', written by Dr. Stephen Bauer, which was posted on the website.

'We're not alone,' I said excitedly to my husband, after reading Barb's bio on the website. There were others out there who have traveled the same path of confusion that we have.

When I read down the list of diagnostic criteria listed in Bauer's paper, the tears welled up in my eyes. My prayers had truly been answered. Now, in front of my own eyes, I had a visual confirmation that I had finally found the complete and correct diagnosis. All the concerns I had about my son were listed there on that page. I thanked God for leading me to the answer that I had long sought.

What surprised both Jim and I was the lack of information about Asperger Syndrome. Although we had found the OASIS website, there was little other information available. I took a trip to my local booksellers and was disappointed to come home empty-handed. I called the local autism society and they sent me a packet of information, which duplicated Barb Kirby's offering. I then called the Autism Society of America and was sent pretty much the same material. I logged on to Compuserve's autism chat area and met some folks online who seemed to be experiencing the same types of things that we were. This was where I first 'met' Tony Attwood, a clinical psychologist in Australia who at the time, was finishing up a manuscript for his book on Asperger Syndrome. His posts in the Compuserve chatroom filled in the holes for many questions I had about Jimmy's behavior. It seemed that I was getting more help via the Internet than I could in my own community.

A month later we took Jimmy for a second opinion. As much as I loathed the whole ordeal it would put him through, I felt it necessary to make absolutely sure that the professionals agreed on Jimmy's diagnosis. I wasn't going to invest the emotional commitment to learning everything there was about an Asperger diagnosis until I had closure from the professionals.

This round of appointments with the doctors was like the start of a new beginning. I approached the three-day regimen with optimism. Jimmy was still anxious in the days leading up to the doctor's visit and was near to nausea on the ride to Philadelphia, but my heart was lighter. I knew that we were headed in the right direction. There was a sense of 'correctness' in my actions this time.

The first day's appointment was a full screening by a developmental pediatrician. The staff at this facility was very understanding of Jimmy's anxiety. I was amazed at the latitude they gave him. If he wanted to have his blood pressure taken in the hallway, they accommodated. When Jimmy became agitated with the sound of an infant's cries in a neighboring room, the nurse somehow managed to move the other family further down the hall, or stop the crying altogether. I was impressed. Exhausting as it was, I was proud of Jimmy. He made it through the whole examination without curling up in the fetal position. However, I also had to give credit to the sensitive staff at the facility. The next day, Jimmy underwent a psychological exam. This time, he would not allow me to leave the room. So I sat directly behind Jimmy while the psychologist gave him a complete IQ test.

On the third day, my husband and I drove into the city for the report on their findings. Again, the diagnosis was Asperger Syndrome. We were relieved. As the doctors presented their reports, we listened as they counseled us to find someone who would teach Jimmy life skills, and to locate another person to counsel Jimmy in social skills, and retain the services of another psychologist just to counsel Jimmy on coping with his disability. They also told us to take him off the Ritalin immediately, as they had noted that the drug had a flattening effect on the personalities of kids like Jimmy, who need every ounce of personality they can muster. I was concerned that they would recommend that we place Jimmy in an educational program for autistic students. Happily, the experts said that what we had been doing in the Communication Handicapped program was the perfect placement all along, and recommended that we continue with the program. Another sigh of relief! The doctors handed us a copy of Dr. Bauer's paper, which again, had been printed off the OASIS website, and sent us on our way. We drove home slightly overwhelmed, but comforted with the knowledge that we had been giving Jimmy the proper care and interventions all along the way. The frustrating part was that we were on our own to find the professionals who could teach social skills, life skills and the other interventions. I would later find that we were not the only parents who would get a diagnosis and a handshake. There is no such thing as one-stop-shopping for services for Asperger Syndrome. Parents are left to their own devices to find, and in many instances create services for their children.

The next several weeks were spent researching Asperger Syndrome. It unnerved me that I was unable to find any information other than what was posted on the OASIS website. I telephoned my HMO for a list of mental health providers. Although they had never heard of Asperger Syndrome, they gave me a list of 12 possible professionals who would take on Jimmy's case. It seemed that the criteria for a HMO referral was whoever handled pediatric cases. I called them all and set up a telephone interview. Based on what I found on OASIS, I had some limited knowledge of what kinds of questions to ask, the first being, 'Are you familiar with Asperger Syndrome?'

I luckily managed to get all 12 professionals on the phone. Only one had heard the term Asperger Syndrome, and he didn't feel as though he was well qualified to take on Jimmy's case. 'Good luck finding help,' he said pleasantly. What he didn't know was he was the last name on my list.

'What are we going to do?' I groused to Jim. 'We have this boy who has a condition that everybody seems to be able to diagnose, but if you ask what to do to help, they have no answers.' I was frustrated. I couldn't believe, in my heart of hearts, that I was stranded on this little sailboat of sorts. There had to be a professional out there who knew and understood what we needed to do.

My husband was the essence of calmness. 'Relax,' he said. 'Remember the doctors said that we were doing all the right things for Jimmy up to this point. The chances of you making any big mistakes are pretty slim. Take your time. Do a thorough search. Something will turn up.'

Later that week, I was in the car on my way to pick up Caroline from school. During that time of day, I usually listened to a talk show called *Fresh Air* on National Public Radio. That day, I heard the flat voice of an author describe her life's experiences as a high functioning autistic. Startled, I turned the volume up on my car radio. Dr. Temple Grandin had just come out with a book called *Thinking In Pictures*, which chronicled her life's struggles. I couldn't believe the serendipity of the discovery. After a week of searching for anything – a book, a video – anything, Temple Grandin chose this time and place to go on a book tour. As I waited in the car for my daughter, I rummaged through my handbag for a scrap of paper to write down the information on her book. I had a pen but could find no paper! In desperation I wrote it all down on my hand. After picking up Caroline and greeting Jimmy off the bus, I immediately drove to the nearest bookseller and found a hardcover copy of the book. Normally I am a cheapskate and would have waited to order the paperback edition, but I was hungry for what waited in its pages. I happily paid the premium price for the hardcover version.

Grandin's book was a revelation to me. For the first time, I could understand the motivation and reasons behind many of my son's behaviors. Her descriptions of sensory issues such as sound and touch provided a whole new perspective. Now I understood why Jimmy put his fingers in his ears when a baby cried! The noise to him was the equivalent of someone running their fingernails against a chalkboard. Now I understood why he avoided rambunctious play! The sensory stimulation was overloading his nervous system! Now I could empathize with my son over his rigidity when it came to clothing choices and food preferences. His skin is ultra sensitive to textures.

Reading Grandin also educated me about the controversies surrounding the whole issue of diagnosing developmental disorders along the autistic spectrum. Apparently I was pretty darn lucky that I got three professionals to agree on the same diagnosis for Jimmy! He could have just as easily been diagnosed with High Functioning Autism, (HFA) or Pervasive Developmental Disorder – not Otherwise Specified (PDD-NOS), which is a fancy term for 'we can't give you an exact diagnosis because the specific criteria don't exist yet – but you still owe us $1,000 for the pleasure of this evaluation.' Or as I heard one researcher describe as being the 'close, but no cigar' diagnosis. I learned the differences between the Kanner-type autism and all the others. Grandin also pointed out to my relief, that individuals with Asperger Syndrome often lead full lives – marriage and gainful employment are not uncommon. Her book was another turning point for me. Thanks to her insights, I now had an insider's view into my son. Now I *could* be sympathetic and compassionate with his bouts of anxiety. This was something up until reading Grandin's work, I could never understand, or be fully patient with.

In the reference section of Grandin's book, I found a wealth of published resources and ran to my nearest bookstore for a copy of *Autism and Asperger Syndrome*, by Uta Frith. This scholarly volume contains Frith's English translation of Hans Asperger's original 1944 doctoral thesis, where he outlines the cluster of behaviors that now bear his name. It was fascinating reading. It is evident that Asperger fully appreciated the wonderful quirkiness of the subjects he wrote so passionately about. In his opening remarks he stressed that these 'exceptional' individuals required 'exceptional' educational programming.

One significant trick that I pulled from his writings was his suggestion of couching all requests in the form of absolute rules, rather than personal requests. It seems that all along, Deanie wasn't far off the mark. I had always found that when I approached Jimmy with ideas in the form of 'rules', I got far better compliance than if I made it known that I wanted something just because it would make mother happy. For example, we always take our dishes away from the table after meals because it is a rule.

Asperger talks a great deal in his paper about educational interventions. Many of his subjects exhibited difficulty in concentration, which was a huge problem for Jimmy. Asperger also noted of the type of instruction that works best with these children is small groups or individual instruction. Anything else seems to overwhelm these children or cause more distraction. I took comfort in knowing that the small classroom setting that Jimmy had been placed in up to this point was validated by Asperger's writings. Asperger notes that these children often take a lot of energy just to do their simple tasks, which explained Jimmy's fatigue. His subjects often went off on another tangent and had to be redirected by the teacher. I made a mental note to share this with Jimmy's teacher, who constantly had to redirect Jimmy back to his work. Now that we knew this was part of the disorder, we could be more patient with him.

There were a few other odd tid-bits that I found interesting in Asperger's paper. He noted that these children often had a 'mature taste' in art. This fit Jimmy's profile. His favorite paintings are Edvard Munch's *Scream* and works by Salvador Dali. He likens himself to Rodin's *Thinker*, and has a poster of the bronze statue hanging in his room. Jimmy also has a taste for Victoriana, particularly Tiffany lamps. Asperger also wrote of the children having a craving for sour foods, which brought back to my mind, the mental image of Jimmy and his grandfather both sitting in the recliner, sucking on those nasty-tasting sour candies. He also tells of the inconsolable homesickness felt by his charges, especially for their mothers. This startled me. Nearly every day, Jimmy would come home from school and tell me how much he missed me. It didn't really mean much to me before. I thought that it was some sort of ritual for him. Was there something more to it? What did this kind of attachment mean? There are days when I feel that I am the only person who truly understands my son. Does he feel the same? Does he cognitively know this although it is unexpressed? Are mothers (or the primary caregiver) the only link to the outside world for kids with Asperger Syndrome?

With all the happiness I experienced with finally getting an answer, I felt some mixture of sadness as well. I could easily see that the odd behaviors Jimmy had were not just a part of his personality, they were rooted in a deeper neurobiological cause. The more I read, the deeper my understanding grew of the battle my son would have to fight for the rest of his life. Up to that point, I have always thought of my son as a little old man trapped in a kid's body. I fully expected that as he grew older, he would grow out of some of his odd behaviors. Now it was very possible that Jimmy would always be an unusual person for the rest of his life. As quickly as the diagnosis of Asperger Syndrome had given me happiness and hope, the enormity of Jimmy's situation was beginning to dawn on me. Now that I had the knowledge of this new mysterious disorder, things had not suddenly changed for the better, the only thing different was that I knew *why* Jimmy behaved the way he did. If I was going to help Jimmy, I would have to do what I had done for the past five years. That was to learn everything there was to learn about this Asperger Syndrome and go from there. I'd done it before with the news about the ADD. Now that I felt I finally had the heart of my artichoke, I could certainly do it one more time.

13

Ch…Ch… Cha… Changes

In the early days of the diagnosis, the only information I found on coping with Asperger Syndrome (and what a little of it there was…) was at conferences dealing with autism. What frustrated me were all the differing opinions on what the disorder was and what caused it. One of the things that irked me was the rush of clinicians who had read a little bit about the disorder, treated one or two patients, and then hit the lecture tour as 'experts'. Some times, it was obvious that the parents in the room knew more about Asperger Syndrome than the speaker. When the presenter would state some ridiculous and erroneous fact, the parents would catch each other's eyes across the room and roll them heavenward, as if to say, 'Obviously this guy hasn't read Christopher Gillberg's work.' Once in a while I'd hear a stifled snicker.

A big bright spot in the morass of ill-informed professionals during those early days was Carol Gray, who is a frequent lecturer on the Social Story concept, which she created as part of her work as an autism consultant to Michigan's Jenison Public Schools in the United States. Carol is a witty and fascinating presenter who has a good sense of humor. Anyone who can get a whole audience singing the theme song from the television comedy show *Laverne and Shirley* as part of their workshop is thinking on my wavelength.

During one conference Carol said something that really clicked with me. She asked the audience if they had ever wondered why our kids ask the same question over and over again. I nodded my head. 'Yes! Carol, Yes!' I was screaming inside. 'Tell me something that'll help me cope with Jimmy's constant questions or I'll go bonkers!'

Carol then described how our kids have a need, almost an obsession for 'sameness'. When we answer their questions with the same answer every time, we are helping them feed their need for sameness. My mind went 'Ka-Ching!' Jackpot! It made perfect sense now! Every time Jimmy asked me a question, he was looking for more than just the answer. He wanted me to reinforce a consistency. It helped him feel grounded. How come I never figured that out sooner? I felt like an idiot. But at least I was an idiot who could now understand the rationale behind the constant barrage of questions ranging from the doctor's office visits to what time his grandmother was coming to dinner.

Before the diagnosis, the questions that came when Jimmy was highly agitated were things I had patience for. In hindsight, these questions came as a result of his need to know what was going to happen next. It was the mundane stuff that really got to me. Perhaps it spawns from Jimmy's craving for sameness *and* his requirement to know what's coming up next. All this repetition was enough to drive me insane. Consider this common exchange:

'Mom?' he would start out. 'What time's dinner?'

'At six-thirty.'

'And is Nanny still coming?'

'Uh-huh.'

'Will Daddy be home too?'

'I think so.'

'What are we eating?'

'Meat, mashed potatoes, corn, salad, and Jell-O.'

We'd go through this about three times and then I'd blow. Even though it was plain to all that I was getting angry at the questions, Jimmy could hardly help himself. He would keep asking.

'Uh, Mom?' he'd ask, his hand up and finger pointed skyward in the 'Caesar pose'.

'Mmmm?'

'Can I ask you one more question?'

'What is it Jimmy?'

'What time is dinner?'

In the past, I would rage at him. 'You just asked me that five minutes ago. I've told you a million times that dinner is at six-thirty! How many times do you want me to tell you that dinner is at six-thirty!' Then he would stalk off and we'd both be in a funk.

After Carol's explanation about the craving for sameness, I was able to better handle the zillions of questions that my son asked. As he got older and better understood my body language and humor, I turned the tables on him.

'Mom?'

'Yes, Jimmy.' This is the third round of questioning. I always gave him two chances to go down his list.

'When's dinner?'

'I forget, what did I tell you?'

'Six-thirty.'

'Oh, OK.'

'And Mom?'

'Uh-huh.'

'Is Nanny still coming?'

'Yes.'

'What are we having for dinner?'

'Oh, ox tails, hummingbird tongues under glass, and snake brains.' I sweetly answered with a highly exaggerated sly-looking expression, which non-verbally spoke, 'get the joke, Jimmy?'

My son stopped dead in his tracks. The next question was ready to come out of his mouth when he did a double take. I waited during the long pause as he thought about what just happened.

'Mom?' he asked, his arms folded in front of him. 'Are you joking with me?'

'Yes. I am Jimmy.'

'Why won't you tell me what's *really* for dinner?'

'Because I already told you what was for dinner,' I said smiling broadly, a kitchen spatula waving in one hand and the other hand on my hip.

'But I like it when you tell me.'

'Lemme tell you what I think,' I said with that 'I've got your number' look. 'You are a boy who likes to ask questions, right?' Jimmy nodded affirmatively. 'And you like to ask Mommy all the same questions over and over, right?' More nodding by my progeny. 'And then I give you the same answers every single time – and you like that, right?'

'Yup' said Jimmy.

'Well, Mommy goes nuts when she has to tell you the same answers all the time. I understand that you just gotta do it. It's like a sneeze. You just got to get it out. So what we're gonna do from now on, is this: When you start asking too many questions, I am going to make up some nonsense silly answers. When I answer your question with something wrong, that sounds like it might be a joke, you'll know that you are asking too many questions. OK?'

'I understand, Mom,' Jimmy nodded solemnly. He always gets so formal when I calmly chew him out. I held back a giggle.

Then with a smirk, he asked 'But can you tell me what's for dinner again?' Then he ran around the corner before I could respond. It just pleases me when we have these breakthroughs. Now, when I give him a quirky answer, he says, 'I know, I know – I'm asking too many questions.'

Dealing with changes has always been a difficult thing for Jimmy. Before we understood his Asperger diagnosis, Jimmy's visceral reactions to some of the household changes would leave us scratching our heads. One time I changed the picture arrangement in our living room and he got violent. It was the first (and only time) he had ever hit me. Although he was a seven-year-old, Jimmy's whack across my back really hurt me. I had no clue why he had such a strong reaction to the new pictures. Before the diagnosis, it just didn't make sense to me. I began to cry in front of my son. He was astonished. In his life, he had never seen his mother so distressed as this and he made the immediate connection. I was simply sobbing my eyes out. In part because my back smarted, on the other part, my heart was broken. To think that my own son could do this to me. Immediate thoughts of his future flooded my eyes through the tears. Children who grow up hitting their mothers are residents of our local jails. My son didn't want to hurt me. I knew that. In my heart, I knew that. Jimmy was a good boy. He just reacted explosively and I was the first thing to punch.

I called my mother. In a dither, I recounted the event and my shock and dismay at what my son had done. 'Was this beginning of a more physical, violent, Jimmy?' I asked her. The thought of him getting in trouble with the law was more than I could bear.

'When things cool down,' my mother counseled, 'You are going to have to sit Jimmy down and explain things to him in very concrete terms why you got so upset. He needs to know the rules for minding himself, and you will have to tell him about the consequences.'

Later that evening, I went into Jimmy's room and closed the door so there weren't any distractions. I began by telling him that he had hurt both my back and my feelings.

'Do you have a rule at school about hitting? I asked.

'Uh huh,' mumbled Jimmy, nodding yes.

'What happens to kids who hit at school?'

'They have to go to the principal's office.'

'Do you know that there are rules about hitting outside of school? I was greeted with a blank stare. There was no connection for him. I then reminded him of his experience earlier that year when the family witnessed someone being hauled off in handcuffs by the police during a domestic violence incident. Back then, I stressed that the reason the police were taking this man to jail was because he was hitting.

'Grownups have a rule about hitting too?' Jimmy asked, creeping deeper into his bed covers.

'Yes son, they do. As you saw, the police take grownups to jail who hit other grownups. It is called 'assault' in police language.

'Do we have a rule about hitting here at home?' I continued.

'No hitting,' he said.

'That's right. Mommy and Daddy don't hit and neither do you kids. It's a rule. Never-ever hit. Do you understand me?' He nodded silently that he did and he never hit me again – although I still had to remind him a few times to take it easy with his sister.

If I thought hanging a few new pictures was going to be bad, all I had to do was wait until we remodeled the house and redecorated the living room. Jim and I had decided that his old recliner had bit the dust. He had bought it before we got married and it was really starting to show battle fatigue. Over the years, I must have mopped up at least 75 baby spit-up stains off the brown velour. My husband, no stranger to spills, had done his share of food faux-pas in the chair, which took its toll. It was time to upgrade. We went to a furniture store and got a great deal on a new green recliner. When it came time to put the old brown chair out with the rubbish, Jimmy became hysterical.

'You can't throw our chair in the trash,' he wailed inconsolably. 'I spent a big part of my "babyhood" in that chair.'

Jim and I looked at each other suddenly. That was perhaps the most passion we had ever heard come out of our son's mouth. Despite the significance, we held back our laughter. Imagine such a fuss and attachment over a ratty old recliner. Jimmy was just a little kid! Visions of the chair-hugging environmentalists popped into my mind, chanting, 'Save the Lazy-Boy! Save the Lazy-Boy!' I had a kid who was attached to a recliner! The gentle pleas of my husband and I had no effect on our son, who dug in. He sat petulantly on the brown chair and turned into a blob of sobbing dead weight.

'You would have thought the dog died,' marveled my husband. 'Let's just wait until after he goes to bed and then we'll just park it out on the curb.'

Jimmy fell asleep in the chair. I felt just awful for him as I carried him off to his room to tuck him into bed, wondering why life's little things are always such a cause of high anxiety for him. Late that night, Jim and I hefted the brown chair outside to the curb. I knew in the morning there would be hell to pay.

As predicted, Jimmy became highly agitated when he looked out the window and saw his beloved recliner out with the trash. The school bus was coming in 15 minutes and I did my best to calm him before he left for school. In the back of my mind, I made a note to call Jim at work after Jimmy was away to school and tease him about leaving me with the hard part of this crisis.

'I hate you!' Jimmy shouted. 'Why are you trashing our chair? It's a part of my life!' Caroline stood off to the side, her eyes the size of tea saucers. I hated the fact that she had to watch this whole angry scene.

How could I argue with my son? It *was* a part of his life. The chair was a source of comfort. His daddy held him in that chair when he was ill. I read him stories like *The Little Engine That Could* until my eyes felt like sand as we sat in that chair. With the imminent arrival of the bus, I left Jimmy at his customary place on the sidewalk and let him deal with his feelings in his own way — privately. I looked from the window as he sat in the chair one last time, talking to himself and patting the chair lovingly. My heart lurched to the bottom of my stomach. Why was this so hard for him? As Jimmy climbed onto the bus that morning, I felt like a total crumb. The next time, I vowed I would ease the pain of the loss somehow. It would be years before I would figure out what was going on in his little head.

Another area where Jimmy's preference for sameness came into play was in his school lunch box. For his mother, who packed his lunch everyday, it was a breeze. No need to rack my brains looking for ways to jazz up his variety. If I even attempted to make a change, it would throw Jimmy off for the rest of the day. In the early years, Jimmy had a peanut butter and jelly sandwich. It had to be made with Skippy brand peanut butter (creamy – not chunky) and Welch's grape jam (not jelly) on white bread, preferably Meier's brand. He would always have a punch flavored juice box, an apple, and a sweet, for which, thankfully, I was allowed some latitude. He ate the same thing every day for years. Most of the time, I got the remains of his lunch back home because he seldom finished what I packed for him. I would constantly query him as to why he didn't eat. Mrs. Fajgier always tried her best to get him to eat. One time, I deduced that he was sick and tired of the same old food day in and day out. So I changed the menu – WRONG! He refused to even touch the food.

His menu only shifted once during elementary school. At the beginning of third grade, one day in desperation, I packed a couple of blueberry muffins that I had freshly baked that morning for breakfast. I knew that Jimmy loved my homemade muffins, made with fresh blueberries. Surely he'd eat them! To everyone's delight, he scarfed them down. From then on, it was blueberry muffins instead of the sandwich. Now one might think that this was an easy situation. I make the muffins, slip them into his lunch and presto! Smooth sailing. Not so. Jimmy would only eat my homemade version. I could not cheat and go to the grocery store bakery aisle and pick up a few to save time. I couldn't even go to the specialty bakery for their expensive muffins. All Jimmy would eat was his Mommy's recipe that had a quarter pound of butter (the real stuff – no substituting), buttermilk, and *fresh* blueberries. When the first winter came, I started to panic. How was I going to find fresh blueberries?! I tried to cheat and got a bag of frozen blueberries at the store. I whipped up a batch and sent them to school in the lunchbox. That night Jimmy came home and said, 'Mom, these muffins are kind of rusty.' His fourth grade teacher said kiddingly, 'If he were my kid, he'd starve.'

I managed to muddle through until the next blueberry season, paying exorbitant prices for imported ones from South America, which required that I hide the grocery bills from my husband. The next year during blueberry season, my mother in law suggested that I buy a flat of berries when they were at the best price, freeze them individually on cookie trays, and bag them up later. This strategy proved to be my saving grace. Jimmy had his blueberry muffins for three straight years, never knowing that the blueberries came from my secret freezer stash.

In what was perhaps the most traumatic scene in Jimmy's life was the day we had to cut down his beloved Mimosa tree. After a year or two of drought conditions, Jimmy's tree, his 'safe spot' had to be cut down. The tree, like many others of the same variety in our neighborhood had been struggling just to grow a few leaves, the next year, it just didn't bloom at all. I was concerned. The tree was now a danger. The next time a strong wind storm cropped up, the tree was likely to topple onto the driveway, damaging the family car, or worse, the house.

I begged my husband not to cut the tree down. I wanted to allow as much time for Jimmy to get used to the idea that his tree was dead. Jimmy always seemed to respect and understand the concept of danger. I just wanted some time to prepare my son.

I bought myself a year. The tree was an eyesore, but I didn't care. The emotion attached to that tree far outweighed the possible danger or the cosmetic gaffe that it was. In my neighborhood of neatly trimmed yards, a dead tree standing on one's front lawn was the equivalent of a pimple on the end of one's nose.

After a year, Jim couldn't put up with Jimmy's dead tree any longer. He was afraid that blowing limbs may damage the cars, or worse yet, Jimmy's continued use of the tree as a perch was a danger. He was older and heavier now and was climbing higher up into the tree. There was a strong possibility that one of the boughs would snap and our son would be badly hurt in a fall. It was time to cut the tree down.

He went to a neighbor's and borrowed a chain saw. While Jimmy was away at school, my husband cut all the limbs off the tree. Out of respect for Jimmy, he left a part of the tree still standing, so that Jimmy could still climb up and sit on part of the stumpy limb. I viewed my husband's efforts as considerate, yet misguided. He should have just cut the whole thing down at once and be done with it. Deal with Jimmy's feelings in one big healing process. By cutting the tree down in two steps, I saw it as dragging out our son's pain. Jimmy would see what was left of the tree as a desecration of his safe spot. Our lawn now sported what looked like a funky piece of modern sculpture. The neighborhood 'pimple' had just transformed into a major zit.

When Jimmy got off the bus that afternoon, he was frantic. There, past the neatly piled wood, was what was left of his tree. Now there was no refuge. He looked at his father and I with hateful eyes. The pain evident as his body nearly shook with rage. I reached my arms out to try and explain but he stormed into his room and slammed the door shut.

'I guess he's really ticked,' said Jim.

'Are we surprised?' I said plaintively. 'We've just taken away his 'safe spot'. I'd say he's more than ticked. He's just been stabbed in the heart by his parents.'

My husband quietly returned the chainsaw to the neighbor's. I went into the house and began the long work of explaining to Jimmy the reasons why we had to cut the tree down. At first he wouldn't open the door. I could have asserted my parental authority and barged in but felt the need to give my son the space. I spoke to him in reassuring tones from the other side of the closed door, explaining to him that while he felt this was a life-altering experience, his feelings would not be as strong over time. Over and over again, I went through the process and rationale that his father and I used to cut down the tree. The discussion struck me as the same kind of approach that a grief counselor would use. Yes! Jimmy was grieving over the loss of his tree. It would be another two years before we could cut the rest of the stump down and cart it away.

Throughout his life, Jimmy has become attached to various things and has never strayed far from them. This has, at times, given cause for much frustration on my part. I had little patience, or understanding for this drive to acquire, or obsession with these objects. It was only after his diagnosis that things made sense to me and I learned that these things fill a vital role in helping to keep Jimmy grounded. These objects provide his life with consistency, comfort, and pleasure. In addition, they gave Jimmy a thread of sameness that helped ease him through the many transitions he needed to make during the day.

We've gone through a couple of distinct phases when it came to the 'objects of Jimmy's obsessions'. The recurring theme is that these things all have to do with the videos, or TV shows that Jimmy watches. Early on, there was the *Sesame Street* phase. Jimmy watched the show at least twice daily. Sometimes, four times a day. He just couldn't be satisfied unless he got the daily dose of his favorite characters. One year, when he was not quite two, I gave him a stuffed 'Big Bird' as a gift for Christmas. This was my first foray into the wonderful world of licensed merchandise. At the time, it seemed like a rather harmless thing. Little did I know that this would set Jimmy off on a life of constant obsession over getting the things that matched the TV shows and videos he watched. He immediately asked me where 'Snuffy' was. Mr. Snuffleupagus is Big Bird's best friend on the *Sesame Street* show. One never went without the other. My only problem was that they didn't start making a stuffed Snuffy for another year. The year Jimmy spent keening for Mr. Snuffleupagus was the mark of things to come.

That same Christmas, my husband's uncle gave Jimmy a set of three die cast trucks that had *Sesame Street* characters for the drivers. If we went anywhere in the car, Jimmy had to have one of the trucks with him. They were his portable objects of obsession. One time, when Jimmy refused to leave the house without his little truck, my husband quipped, 'It's just like the American Express commercial, 'don't leave home without it."

I remember the time I took Jimmy to the grocery store and he lost his little green truck. He became frantic. My grocery cart was loaded with perishables, I was ready to head for the checkout line, and I stupidly told Jimmy that he'd just have to be more careful with his toys. He became frantic. So much for trying to save my ice cream from melting. Jimmy started to wail like a banshee, a panic in his eyes that unnerved me. We had to find the little green truck or it would take a week or more to recover. With a prayer in my heart, we searched every aisle of the store. I sheepishly asked some of the store personnel for assistance. After 20 minutes one of the store clerks found the green truck nestled in the display of under ripe green bananas. It was a miracle. The bananas proved to be the perfect camouflage for the truck. I still credit divine intervention for that find.

Like just about everybody else on the planet, Jim and I took the kids to see Disney's *Toy Story*. This movie would immediately replace *Thomas the Tank Engine* as Jimmy's all consuming interest. Jimmy had to have everything that was connected in any way with the movie. Thanks to Disney's marketing and merchandizing juggernaut, there were plenty of objects to obsess over. Jimmy's 'Woody' doll was his constant companion for the next several years. He dragged that doll everywhere. We never left the house without it. Like the character in the storyline, Jimmy wrote his own name on the bottom of Woody's cowboy boot – just like it happened in the movie.

When Jimmy was little, it was kind of cute to see him packing his Woody doll everywhere. When he got older, it got to be very conspicuous and I had the heartbreaking task of telling him that Woody had to stay back. I picked a time when Jimmy and I were alone in the car. As usual, Woody was along for the ride. As I parked and got ready to walk into the grocery store, Jimmy grabbed Woody.

'How about it if Woody stays in the car?' I asked.

'But he always comes along with me.'

'I know,' I said gently, my mind searching for a good way to break the sad news. 'You know, we really need to have a talk about

Woody. You are a ten-year-old now and all the boys don't carry dolls around when they go to the store.'

By luck a group of adolescents happened to be walking past the car, headed towards a pizza place. Jimmy looked at them.

'See,' I said softly. 'None of those boys is carrying a Woody doll, or any other toy.'

'What should I do?' Jimmy asked. He really had no clue how to deal with this new development – growing up.

'Well, I think that it's not a good idea for you to take Woody inside the store anymore. I didn't tell you this before but I saw some kids laughing at you last time because you had Woody with you,' I confessed.

Jimmy looked sad. 'I don't want any kids laughing at me.'

'I don't either. But I have an idea for you. How about bringing Woody in the car and when we go into the store, he can sit and wait for us. That way the kids won't laugh at you and Woody won't get lost like he did in the movie. I promise to lock the car and keep the windows closed. The suggestion seemed to please Jimmy and we followed this protocol for several months. By the time he was eleven, he outgrew the whole *Toy Story* thing completely – but it was substituted with an obsession for *Speed Racer*, a passion that is far more age-appropriate and socially acceptable. And what is now the object of his obsession? A *Speed Racer* baseball cap. Jimmy never leaves home without it.

14

Making Sense of the Sensory

Recently, Jimmy pulled a piece of paper out of his pocket, unfolded it and took a deep sniff. The scrap had been given to him by a former teacher from his elementary school and Jimmy had recently gone to visit because he was missing all the old friends he left there. The teacher had jotted down her e-mail address so the two of them could correspond. The whiff of his old school had its intended effect. Jimmy's face brightened and he said, 'Ahh, that reminds me of my good ole school.'

Jimmy has always had a pernickety nose. His olfactory senses are somehow affected with a heightened sensitivity that often leaves me scratching my head. As a baby, the first thing he did when opening a book was hold it up close to his face and take in a deep breath. My husband once said that Jimmy took the term 'sticking your nose into a book' to whole new heights. The look of pleasure on his face when he did this was a nice departure from the familiar stoic scowl that we normally saw.

Jimmy is always aware of the scent of his environment. One time, we were in a store and he commented how one room smelled like his grandmother's house. He equates the smell of coffee in certain settings with an airport. If you forget to brush your teeth, he'll spot the halitosis a mile away and tell you that you have bad breath.

Sometimes certain foods can set him off. I recall a large family dinner at Nanny's house. The table was set with fine linens and china. All the family gathered around to sit down. Nanny placed a last-minute casserole dish of candied yams near Jimmy's customary spot. Everyone sat down and clasped hands to begin the prayer over the food.

'Nanny?' said Jimmy, 'Can you move this? I'm sorry, but it just doesn't agree with my nose.' Knowing how sensitive his schnozzer is, Nanny quickly obliged. We were pleased with his request. When he was younger, he would have protested in a more unacceptable way.

One of the more fascinating anecdotes about Jimmy's keen sense of smell is a story my father related to me during one of his visits. One afternoon, Daddy sat on the porch and read the paper as the kids played. Jimmy was only a seven-year-old at the time. Caroline was involved with some neighborhood girls. Presently some little boys who had just moved into the house down the street stopped by for a rare visit. They saw Jimmy was playing with his *Star Wars* action figures and ran home to get their own collection.

When the playtime was over and it was time to separate the toys and send the boys home, my father tells me of a remarkable occurrence. It seemed that there were two Luke Skywalker action figures. The boys paused, not knowing which Luke belonged to whom. To solve the dilemma, my father said that Jimmy held each one up to his nose, took a quick sniff, and immediately told the other boy, 'this one is yours'.

After Jimmy got older, he would come up to me from behind, put his arms around my neck and sniff my hair. When I would ask him what he was doing, Jimmy would simply say, 'I'm remembering you.' At times I would catch him bending over his sister and lightly sniffing her hair.

'What are you doing?'

'I'm sniffing Caroline.'

'Why?'

'Her hair smells good.'

'You like to sniff a lot don't you?' I said, stating the obvious.

'Uh huh.'

'Do you sniff like this at school?' I asked, a nightmare flashing through my mind of the principal calling me in for a conference to put a stop to my son from sniffing all the girls' hair.

'No.'

'That's good,' I said. 'You know there's a rule. You don't sniff people without their permission.' This social rule was pretty obvious too. But with Jimmy, you never knew. He had to hear all these little social codes verbally – as rules – so he knew what the world expected of him. I always gave him 'the rule' for everything; hoping for the day he would roll his eyes heavenward as if to say, 'Do I look like an idiot? Of course I know that Mom.' Sadly, those 'Duh, Mom' looks came far and few between. Maybe all his sniffing might someday lead Jimmy into a lucrative career as a lab technician in a perfume factory.

The nose sensitivity was nothing compared to the tactile sensitivity. This was a cause of some stress in our home. One night after dinner, I noticed that my husband seemed unusually down. Something was bothering him. I opened up a discussion with, 'Care to tell me what's on your mind?'

'It's Jimmy,' he said. 'I just get the feeling that he doesn't like me. When I come home from work, Caroline comes running for a big hug, but Jimmy couldn't care less that I'm alive. If anything, he runs away when he sees me coming in the door.'

I could see that Jim was hurting. By all accounts, Jimmy's lack of interest in his father's arrival each night would lead most to think that the son just didn't care about his Daddy. This wasn't the first time he'd mentioned this concern to me. As I sat at the kitchen table, the thought came into my head that Jim was right – his son *was* trying to avoid him. But why?

'Oh, honey,' I soothed. 'We know Jimmy is almost the exact opposite of his sister. Maybe it's just his way. Maybe he's got a Greta Garbo complex, you know – "*I vant to be alone.*"'

For the next week, I watched the interactions between Jim and Jimmy. After a couple of days, it was plain to me that what we were suffering from was a case of avoidance due to overstimulation. I observed Jim as he played with Caroline. She would jump into his arms and they would poke at each other and tickle, as most loving demonstrative parents and kids will do. One time, I counted seven kisses exchanged between the two of them in a 20-second period. They engaged in the typical huggy-touchy-tickly type stuff, perfectly normal by anyone's standards.

Enter Jimmy. As soon as the opportunity presented itself, Jim would grab Jimmy and give him a big hug, squeezing tightly, all the while he would be talking loudly about how much be missed his son while he was at work, asking him how school went, and what was for supper. Then he would start to ruffle up his hair with a good-old fashioned 'noogie' and then start in with the tickling. Moments later, Jim would become upset and offended when his son pushed away. He hardly got in any time for even a little kiss.

'You see!?' Jim said as Jimmy stalked away. 'Why won't he come to me?! He'll sit on *your* lap.' Everyone's feelings were hurt and a foul mood invaded the house. Again, the conversation at the dinner table would be quiet.

As time went on, the problem became obvious to me. When I looked at the situation from the perspective of my son it became clear why he was actively avoiding his father. He was being bombarded. Jimmy didn't feel 'safe' with his father.

'I think I've got this figured out,' I said to my husband. 'I hope you take this in the spirit with which it is intended, but you are right, Jimmy is avoiding you. But there is a very good reason why.' I started to explain to my husband that Jimmy couldn't handle all the sensory stimuli that he perceived as part of the package when Daddy was around the house. I told him the even a simple hug was even too much for our son.

'He feels like he's getting chewed up and spit out after a session with you,' I said in hushed tones, not wanting the children to hear. 'Jimmy doesn't feel "safe" with you.'

'That's ridiculous!' scoffed my husband.

'Try to understand it from Jimmy's point of view! He just goes on overload, and rather than get into confrontation because he's been taught to be polite, he just does an end-run.' I watched my husband's face. The hurt was there, but I also saw his understanding that his parenting approach would have to be different with his son. One size does not fit all – even in houses where the children are typical.

At that moment, Jimmy walked into the kitchen. 'Now don't say anything; just watch.' I wanted to give my husband an idea of just how much he would have to cut back on the demonstrative behavior.

'Hey Jimmy!' I called. 'Come here. I need a hug.' Jimmy warily eyed his father, who was sitting nearby. He walked around the table, deliberately avoiding a possible snare, and sat on my lap. With my hands at my sides, I waited as Jimmy sort of fell limp against my chest and put his head on my neck in a sort of little nuzzle. There was no embrace. Over my son's shoulder, I silently mouthed to my husband, 'See!' When Jimmy felt the 'hugless hug' was sufficient, he silently got up and made his way back to the TV.

'That's it?' asked my husband, his voice a mix of incredulity and sheepishness. In the beginning, Jim still didn't quite grasp the underlying basis for the hands-off approach, but in time, he would come to understand that his son's needs were far more specialized than he had known. Later, he would take Jimmy aside and explain to him what he thought had happened. Then he would go on to tell Jimmy that no longer would he be so grabby and loud. He promised his son that he would try hard to respect his need for a more quiet way of showing affection. And it worked! Within three weeks, Jimmy was more responsive to his father. The 'hugless hug' technique helped bring father and son closer together. Jimmy finally felt 'safe' with his father.

Over time, it would become more apparent that our son was like a wild deer, whose flight instinct had a hair trigger. This would require great understanding and patience on all our part. This facet of our son's make-up had the propensity to impact most, if not all, the activities of the family. I recall the first time we took the children ice-skating at a nearby rink. Caroline was so excited and could hardly wait to lace up her ice skates. For the rest of us, the evening proved to be exhausting.

When we arrived at the rink, the final period was still ongoing for a local ice hockey tournament. We were allowed to go into the ice area and sit on some bleachers for an up-close view of the action. Our family had never ever been to see live action hockey and it was a very noisy, very exciting thing to watch. Players were 'checking' each other, referees were constantly tweeting their whistles, and the loudspeaker was blaring. There was blood, cursing, and all the other violent things that make up a hockey game. Jimmy sat transfixed, shivering in the cold, his hands over his ears. He was fascinated with the new experience, yet I could see that it was hard for him to handle. I kept promising him that it would soon be over, to watch the scoreboard clock and then we could enjoy some nice ice-skating.

When it came time for the general public to go onto the ice, Jimmy refused, and insisted that no one else in the family do either. 'It's a very dangerous place, you can't go!' he implored. It was clear that he wouldn't shake the rough images of the hockey team. In his mind, anyone who went out on the ice would be roughed up, bloodied, and will have a referee blow a whistle at them. Any thoughts of a genteel spin on the ice to the tunes of a soothing Strauss waltz were not in his mind's eye.

My husband and I were torn. We had two children. Caroline's needs had to be considered too. She had been looking forward to this outing for weeks. She talked about it excitedly for days in anticipation. Many times, a family plan was called off because it didn't mesh with Jimmy's capacity to handle a situation. Now here we were, at the rink, we've already paid our money for the skate rental. It would have devastated our daughter to have to pack up and go home. We decided to stick it out and let the chips fall where they may. If Jimmy acted out, let the public stare.

Jimmy was incensed that we would let his little sister do such a dangerous thing. We all stood by the rink side door and watched Caroline skate by herself. The smile on her face was worth all the aggravation that Jimmy was about to give us.

'You can't let her go out there, she's going to get hurt!' Jimmy wailed at us.

He started pounding on the Plexiglas barrier surrounding the rink. Jim started to stop him. I waved him off saying, 'He's not going to do any damage to Plexiglas.' So for the next hour, we proudly watched our little one skate solo around the rink, which made Jimmy literally climb the walls. I had never thought it possible to witness someone in the act of climbing the walls, but Jimmy was doing just that. My son was frantic. We tried to point out how happy his sister looked. It seemed to help calm him. What wasn't helping was the loud rock music blaring from the loud speakers and the freezing temperatures inside the rink. Thankfully, it was so loud that Jimmy's antics failed to draw much attention from the crowd. Jim and I steeled ourselves and just let things go. This time our daughter's needs would take precedence over our son's. I offered to take Jimmy to the warm snack bar area, but he refused. He didn't want to miss any possible disaster to his sister.

'Are we having fun yet?' asked my husband with a sly grin. I punched him in the shoulder with a smirk. When the evening was over, we all arrived home tired, with mixed emotions. Caroline had thoroughly enjoyed her time on the ice, Jim and I were happy that we had made it through another 'adventure', and Jimmy was glad his sister wasn't killed or maimed. The next day, Debbie would tell me that Jimmy had a lot to talk about in his speech class. At least there was one silver lining to that cloudy ordeal.

Jimmy's hypersensitivity to his clothing and other fabrics has always been a challenge. I could never figure out if he was more obsessed with having things always be the same, or if the 'feel' of the clothing was what he preferred over everything else – or if it was both! Once he found an article of clothing that he liked to wear, I had to make sure that we had plenty of them on hand. For years, the only white athletic socks that Jimmy would wear came from the Mervyns stores that were in the western United States. I had to send my mother out for socks when Jimmy wore holes in the ones he had. As he grew, I would just buy the next size up. The problem came when Jimmy's feet outgrew the socks the store carried in that style. We tried just about every other store brand imaginable – even flea market offerings. It looked as though Jimmy would be wearing shreds until we lucked out with a sock sold through a discount store chain.

During the winters, Jimmy, like his grandfather, insisted on wearing flannel shirts. Again, I couldn't stop the progress of time and after a year, Jimmy outgrew his favorite shirts. He was loath to try new shirts, and at the same time, he was clearly uncomfortable in the ones that now were too small. Jimmy wouldn't let me take the clothes that were too small out of his closet and hand them down to his sister. I'd have to wait until they were two sizes too small and then sneak them out to the Salvation Army.

Especially when he was younger, there often were times when we would have knockdown, drag-out fights over fussiness with Jimmy's clothing. Often, both he and I would be in tears. Thankfully, I found one solution in the Lands' End clothing company. I had shopped out of this catalog for myself on many occasions, finding their clothing to be well made. I bought some flannel shirts for Jimmy and was pleased with how well they survived the washing machine. When he outgrew his favorite green plaid shirt, I could simply go to the catalog and buy the next size up.

I also had some luck shopping with Jimmy at the rummage and second-hand shops. On one occasion, the school was having a Hawaiian luau party and the children were invited to wear festive clothing appropriate to a luau. In desperation, I drove Jimmy over to a second hand shop to look for anything that smacked of Hawaii.

I had originally discovered the value of going second-hand when Jimmy became obsessed with obtaining a necktie exactly like the one worn by the character in the movie *James and the Giant Peach*. I was tickled that the pennies I spent for the knit necktie brought such peace back to the house. Jimmy and I searched the kids size racks for anything Hawaiian. There was nothing. On the way out, we scanned through the selection in the men's sizes. There it was! The perfect shirt. Although it was a size small, it still fit. To this day, it is still one of his favorite shirts. Now, Jimmy and I hit the second-hand shops on a regular basis.

Jimmy insisted on wearing the same style fleece sweat pants every day to school. They were the same style of pants that his grandfather favored after work hours. Jimmy calls them 'Pop Pants'. I thought my son was doomed to a life of jockish sloppiness, until the summer after his year in elementary school. On a whim, Jimmy enrolled in a camp for performing arts that had been suggested by the school psychologist. It was three weeks of daylong theater workshops at a local community college. Although the program was well supervised, I had to get over my angst of dropping my son off at a college campus every morning. I wondered if he would find his way. Each workshop was located in a different room, some in different buildings. Lunch was eaten in the student union building. It was the perfect opportunity for Jimmy to get exposed to the idea of rotating for classes, and since middle school was coming up in the fall, I felt the need to let him give it a try.

The last week of the camp was spent in rehearsals for a final performance, a Broadway-style song and dance revue. To my utter chagrin, Jimmy had opted for the dance segment of the camp and his group would be performing a free-form number reminiscent of the 'Sharks and Jets' scene in the musical *West Side Story*. His costume was a white T shirt and a pair of denim pants, which the camp director figured would be a staple in every kid's wardrobe. Jimmy hadn't owned a pair of denim pants since they were given as a gift at his baby shower. I worried that he would be unable to participate in the show because he wouldn't be able to wear the costume.

'It says here that your costume is a white T-shirt and a pair of blue jeans,' I read from the wardrobe sheet to Jimmy, the day before the final performance. 'Do you have any jeans?' I asked, knowing the answer would be negative.

'What should we do?'

'We *have* to have this for the performance,' Jimmy said. For him, this costume, although mundane, was a fact set in concrete – a rule. 'Can you take me to the store for some jeans?'

I had waited 12 long years to hear those words. We jumped into the car and headed for the nearest shopping mall. I wasn't going to give Jimmy any time to think about the implications of what he just said. We arrived at the department store with the plastic charge card warming up in my hot little hand. Most adolescent boys hate to shop for clothing and Jimmy is no exception. I made the trip as short and sweet as possible. We found his size, tried the pants on, and BINGO! We were out of there in less than 10 minutes. On the drive home, I wondered if I just blew our hard-earned money on a pair of pants that would be worn only once. At the very least, I would take a photo to honor the momentous occasion.

On the night of the performance, Jimmy did very well. I was absolutely beaming at my son from my seat way, way up in the nosebleed section of the theater. I tried not to let anyone see the tears of a proud mother slipping down my face for fear that they would think I was nuts.

After the performance, Jimmy wanted to attend the cast party. We went home so he could shower and change. When he was ready to leave, I was shocked to see him wearing the blue jeans.

'You look nice,' I said nonchalantly, but inside my heart was soaring.

'Thanks, Mom,' said Jimmy, who in my eyes had suddenly shed his childlike aura. Standing before me was a young man, who for the first time in his life, had voluntarily chosen to dress appropriately for the occasion. After years of struggling with his preference for sameness, Jimmy had taken the big step and ventured outside the box. I felt like Cinderella's fairy godmother. Even if he wore those blue jeans for just one night, there was no discounting the significance of Jimmy's choice. It was a huge breakthrough.

That fall, Jimmy would choose again to venture outside his comfort zone. On the first day of school, he wore the blue jeans. His beloved fleece pants were relegated to the bottom drawer of his bureau, only worn for lounging around on weekends. Jim took me aside one September evening and commented on how proud he was of Jimmy.

'He really has made a big step towards growing up,' Jim marveled. 'The new blue jeans really make him look his age now.'

'I know what you mean,' I said. 'It's as though he's aged five years overnight!' With Jimmy, progress is always slow in coming, but when the breakthroughs happen, they are like leaps in his life. As his parents, we remember each of his milestones with the same intensity and appreciation as the memories of our own significant life events such as a first kiss, or wedding ceremony, or birth of a child. Our son has had to go through so much extra effort to achieve these seemingly mundane life skills. The details of these accomplishments can't help but be burned in our memory.

15

Holla-daze

I remember having to sit in many a doctor's waiting room during the holiday season, thumbing through one of the well-worn women's magazines that littered the tables. I grimly scanned the table of contents for a clue as to what lay inside for me: the mother of a kid with a developmental disability. What could they say that would have meaning or benefit for me? One of the things I noticed was the recurring theme: 'Relieve Your Holiday Stress!'

'Sure,' I harrumphed to myself, noting the 'tips' in the magazine always included the suggestion, 'Try something new.'

Not at my house. Obviously these magazine editors had never dealt with a child who became so overwhelmed by the constant transitions involved in opening his Christmas gifts, that he would get to the point where he would just shut down inside and stare into space. How many of them have a son who would not allow anyone to sing 'Happy Birthday', not only at his own birthday, but with everyone else in the family too? Or would go into a black hole at school after returning from a two-week holiday break because he couldn't make the transition? Holiday stress? Let's talk about holiday stress. My way of dealing with stress is a nice pound-box of my favorite See's chocolates. After all, isn't S-T-R-E-S-S-E-D, when spelled backwards, D-E-S-S-E-R-T-S? Just keep passing me those Christmas cookies, and I'll make it through the holiday hassles just fine, thank you.

Jimmy's condition has impacted our family's celebrations of all special occasions in a particular way. Sure, we celebrate, just like everyone else does. But with special considerations and modifications, a little here, a little there; not enough for us to feel like we're missing anything that others are doing. Yet, when you think about all the little things where Jimmy's quirks had to be accommodated, it's quite exhausting.

Take Halloween for example. Halloween has been near torture every single year of my son's life. Getting through Halloween with Jimmy was like running the Boston Marathon in stiletto heels. The month-long struggle began when the first bags of stale candy appeared in the grocery store, and would end in my living room on Hallows Eve with my frustrated kid throwing his flashlight and a virtually empty sack of candy on the floor in disgust. I like to call the holiday 'Hell-oween'.

The first issue I had to deal with was selecting the costume that he would wear to 'Trick or Treat'. Early on, things were easy. Jimmy was Spiderman the first two years and Superman for the second two. After he entered school, Jimmy always obsessed over what he would wear for up to a year in advance. He always had to be a superhero. I never heard other mothers in the neighborhood having to suffer through months of constant angst over the exact details of their kid's Halloween costume. It was a disaster when it came time to buy the costume and the superhero of choice did not come in his size or was nowhere to be found. Sometimes the sensory issues got in the way.

One year Jimmy had obsessed for months about dressing up as 'The Mask', a character made famous by the actor Jim Carrey. Jimmy had looked forward in the worst way to wearing his costume. Luckily I was able to find it that year, and it did not come cheap. When it came time to prepare to go out, things quickly deteriorated. Jimmy dressed in his costume only to find that he couldn't stand the feeling of it on his skin. I watched in surreal shock as he literally clawed the costume off his body. As he looked at the pile of brightly colored fabric at his feet and realized that there was no way he could wear the costume that he had anticipated wearing for months, the frustration and disappointment were clearly evident on his face. Why, oh why, were the simplest pleasures such a difficult thing for my sweet son?! My heart broke to see Jimmy's pain. I hated Halloween.

One year, I was fretting to some other parents about the scarcity of a Sonic the Hedgehog costume in a size seven. I had been to several stores in a tri-county area only to come up empty handed. One of the mothers looked at me like I was an idiot and suggested substituting one of the Super Mario Brothers in its place. I didn't bother trying to explain that substitution was not an option for a child with Asperger Syndrome. It would do no good to even try. I would only end up sounding like the over- indulgent mother who would move heaven and earth to get her spoiled son what he wanted. I bit my tongue and held it all in.

The actual canvassing for candy was always a nightmare. My son always wanted to go out and knock on the neighborhood doors so badly, yet he could hardly bring himself to do it. At issue for him was the big unknown. Jimmy rarely went to these homes and didn't know what to expect when he rang the doorbell. He also would not go to any house that had a dog – especially a barking dog.

So there we would be, year after year, shivering in the cold night air, debating whether or not to ring up someone's house. Very often Jimmy would send Caroline with his treat bag to collect his candy while he stood 'safely' at the edge of the driveway. It was very frustrating – especially to my husband, who in time, would understand why it was nearly impossible for his son to enjoy a seemingly normal activity like 'Trick or Treating' – a right of passage for every American child. As tough as we all knew it would be for Jimmy, we did our best to understand and accommodate his needs. Sometimes, the neighbors who knew of Jimmy's difficulties were kind enough to offer extra candy to Caroline, knowing that her frustrated brother was standing at the end of their driveway, too scared of the unknown, or overwhelmed by their pet, to muster up the courage to stand on their door step.

All the way along, I told Jimmy, 'When you turn 12, there is no more "Trick or Treating".' I simply set this fact out as a given, not subject to any negotiation. The day of his 12th birthday the first thing he said when he awakened was, 'I guess I don't get to go "Trick or Treat" anymore.' That year, he answered the door and handed out the candy to all the little ghosts and goblins that came. The memory of a two-year-old Jimmy paralyzed with fear at the strange sight of scary-looking characters arriving at his door was long gone. That first Halloween when Jimmy stayed home was a pure pleasure for me. My husband took out Caroline and she enjoyed not having to deal with her brother's fears. Her sack of candy intake doubled because she was able to move freely about the neighborhood. There was no debate over each house that was approached. She could simply go up and ring the bell. Jimmy seemed happier at home, helping me dole out the candy, and I was thrilled just to have a hassle-free Halloween.

We may have been able to 'graduate' from Halloween, but we'll never be able to say the same for the Christmas holiday – not that we'd ever want to. After 12 years, by trial and error, we were able to figure out the mistakes that we made and make the time a more enjoyable one.

When Jimmy was little, my husband and I both noticed that he didn't seem to be himself on Christmas morning. He enjoyed the festivities, like all children do, but we could never quite put our finger on why he seemed so distracted and lethargic. There were times when he would just sit, surrounded by shreds of wrapping paper and stare off into space. He didn't seem to enjoy all the gifts, which was odd considering that he nearly drove himself bonkers with anticipation before the 24th of December. One year it was obvious that my husband was offended because, in his mind, Jimmy didn't appreciate all the nice gifts he had received.

After we had gotten Jimmy's Asperger diagnosis and I had read some research into the difficulty that some kids have in making transitions, the idea just popped into my mind as I watched Caroline foist yet another wrapped box under Jimmy's nose on Christmas morning. Jimmy's response was flat. It 'appeared' as if he wasn't interested. But on a closer look, the thought that Jimmy was getting close to overload was something I couldn't shake. Every box that he was given required that he re-set his thoughts and make a transition. Ding! The little light went on in my head. We were bombarding Jimmy with too many stimuli, albeit good stimuli. My son couldn't handle the load. I silently motioned to my husband to leave Jimmy alone for a while, to just let him enjoy the toys he was currently playing with. When I had the chance, I took Jim aside and explained my theory. He agreed that it sounded plausible and we observed for the rest of the morning.

'Yup, we're definitely on overload,' he later said. We agreed that we needed to re-think our gift-giving strategy. After a year or two of tinkering, we both found that less is more in Jimmy's case. We would set our budget, and buy more expensive items so that he would have half as many packages to open on Christmas morning. Later, I found that wrapping only half the gifts helped. It lessened the angst over the terrible unknown that is a particular problem for kids with Asperger Syndrome. I would set out the items that Santa Claus had brought unwrapped. Gifts from family members would be wrapped.

There always comes a time when a parent must tell their child that Santa is make-believe. Most of the time, kids pretty much know the truth by the time they are nine. In Jimmy's case, he still appeared to be a believer at age ten. Caroline asked me for a confirmation of the Santa rumor at age eight. Since Jimmy was running the risk of embarrassing himself with his schoolmates should the issue of Santa's existence come up for discussion, I felt it was best to clue him in. Part of me thought that Jimmy really knew that Mommy and Daddy played the part of Santa and just didn't want to hurt our feelings by bringing it up. The other part knew of my son's anticipation of Santa's upcoming arrival. He constantly talked of Santa. Was he baiting me?

One day, I decided to take the plunge. Jimmy and I were riding in the car on an errand. As we pulled into the driveway, Jimmy asked me a question about Santa's source of toys.

'You know who does all the Santa shopping, don't you?' I asked tentatively.

'The elves?'

'No,' I said looking at him.

'It's Mommy.'

'I wondered how Santa knew exactly what we wanted,' said Jimmy with an expression that puzzled me. I thought he would be hurt to know the truth. I relaxed. This was going to be a piece of cake.

'So how do you get everything to the North Pole?' he asked.

'Honey, I don't send stuff to the North Pole,' I said, wondering what was going on in his mind. 'I stuff it up in the attic and in the trunk of Daddy's car.'

'But how do you fit all the toys for all the kids in the world in our attic? Where do you keep the sleigh?'

I sat stunned. Obviously I was being too subtle for Jimmy. I felt like such a bumbler. Now, to set the record straight, I would have to be blunt, cold and to the point. My stomach felt queasy.

'Do you think Mommy is the Santa Shopper for all the kids in the world?' I asked. 'No, I only shop for you and your sister.' Now Jimmy's expression made sense. He thought I *was* Santa. I was angry with myself, thinking that I had really put my foot in my mouth this time. Here I was, making the biggest goof of all time during one of the most important 'coming clean' chats that parents have with their children, save the discussion that follows the question about the sperm and the egg.

'Wait a minute!' said Jimmy, his brow knitted, finger raised in the Caesar pose. 'You're telling me that there *is* no Santa Claus?!'

'There is no Santa Claus. Mommy has been doing it,' I winced internally.

'But you have been telling me about the elves and the North Pole and Mrs. Claus, and the sleigh with eight tiny reindeer,' Jimmy said accusatorily. 'You lied to me all these years! Now, I'll never get the Christmas spirit again!'

The hurt and sadness that I was expecting did not happen. All I could gauge from Jimmy's reaction was his anger at being lied to. I was totally taken by surprise. This kind of response I had not imagined. I had anticipated hurt feelings, but not anger. There was nothing I could really say. I *had* lied to him. All parents lie about Santa to their children. Jimmy's world was so black and white. Either there was a Santa, or their wasn't. I felt as though I had permanently violated my child's trust.

'So there is not God or Jesus either,' said Jimmy sarcastically, pounding his fist into the window of the car. 'You made that up too so I would go to church.'

I wanted to vomit. The reasoning was a natural progression. All of us believe in our respective deity strictly on faith. Children never see Santa delivering the goods. They too, believe in the idea of a jolly old elf strictly on faith. Jimmy immediately recognized the parallels. My skin crawled. What had I done?! My faith was a guiding force in my life. I wanted it to be the same for my children. To hear my own son speculate on the lack of God's existence was abhorrent to me. And the thought that this was a result of my own deception was making me light-headed.

'Son,' I said, reaching for his hands. 'Mommy wants you to know that God and Jesus are real. I would never lie to you about them.' Somehow the words I had just spoken seemed hollow. 'Santa is a fairy tale that grown-ups make up for their children to bring them happiness through giving. Now that you know the truth about Santa, it will be your turn to bring a child happiness by giving gifts.' Jimmy and I talked for several more minutes. I poured my heart out to him about my conviction of the reality of God's existence and his Son Jesus. Then, I invited Jimmy to help me with the year's preparations. That evening, Jimmy went to bed by himself. I felt as though I was being shut out. His hurt and anger with me would last nearly a fortnight. Later, I would have to clue him in on the Easter Bunny and the Tooth Fairy. Oddly, he made the connection with Santa and deity, but not the bunny and the fairy.

Family vacations away from home are always a challenge for the family that has a child with Asperger Syndrome. Jimmy always complains how his life is so boring, yet, when you introduce a change – even a positive one – the effect is stressful. Once a year, we try to fly to my parents', a five-hour ordeal of toll roads, airports, baggage claim, and new surroundings. Jimmy enjoys going to his grandparents' home, nestled in the heart of the Wasatch Mountains of Utah, in the western United States. It seems like every year we travel, it gets easier for Jimmy because he knows the routine. However, it was not always Easy Street. When he was little, Jimmy would obsess about the trip to Grandma and Grandpa's house, talking about nothing else until we were all ready to muzzle him. One year, I took the kids on the long flight in. Unfortunately we had several mishaps, delayed connecting flights, lost luggage, and just about everything went wrong. It was two in the morning when we arrived safely at my folk's place. Considering the time zone difference, it was four in the morning. The kids were exhausted. As soon as he sat down in the sofa, Jimmy started to cry.

'I want to go home,' he started to wail.

I looked incredulously at my parents and burst out laughing. I had just fought the Battle of the Bulging Suitcase, spent nine hours with two youngsters in various airports, and a host of other ills, just to get to my parents' house. Now, after 90 seconds, my son wants to go home?! This was ludicrous. Jimmy needed time to make the transition and he was exhausted. After a trip with Grandpa into the kitchen for milk and cookies, we went to bed and would make the adjustment the next day.

On one of our trips to my parents in recent years, the state was having a very big festival, a sesquicentennial celebration of the Mormon pioneers' trek across the American Great Plains and entrance into the Salt Lake Valley. I was very much looking forward to visiting the state and taking in everything that the organizers of the celebration had to offer. In a strong sense, I was looking at the weeklong celebration as a way to return to my own childhood through many of the events that were annually staged to commemorate the July 24 event. Only this year, there was much, much, more to do.

I took the kids everywhere: parades, concerts, balloon races. We took it all in a little at a time. My sister helped me manage both of the kids, especially when I needed to take Jimmy aside to gather himself together and get a little quiet time. On the last day of the celebration, I took the kids to a large fair. There were displays of antique ox-carts, log cabins built on the premises and historic interpreters dressed in period costume. We had been to a Civil War festival similar to this one in our hometown, only this one was much larger. I didn't think the fair would present any problems for Jimmy, who was looking forward to it as much as I.

The trip was a disaster. The fair proved to be noisy, hot and crowded. Live animals spooked Jimmy. He went on overload within minutes. Our car was parked a five minutes' walk away. It wasn't such an easy thing to change our minds and go back to the car. More important, I had traveled halfway across the continent to see some of the displays at this festival. I didn't want to leave. Against my better judgement, I dug in and dragged the kids all around.

When we got to the Indian Pow-Wow dance, Jimmy shut down. The banging drums, jingling bells, smoke from the camp fire, and chanting was all too much for him. Not only that, the colorful costumes and heat of the day seemed to stress his other senses. He had a melt down, unlike the others I had seen. Usually he turns inward and goes flaccid when he is overstimulated. This time he started to act out. He began lashing out at me verbally and physically, tugging on my arms, pushing me in the direction of the car. I looked searchingly at my mother and sister, who were with us on the trip. A mixture of emotions swept through my mind. I wanted to stay. I had looked forward to this event for some time. What about what 'I' want!? At the same time, I knew that there was no way Jimmy could handle it. A wave of disgust and anger crashed through me as my sister reached into her handbag for her car keys. I was deeply disappointed that I couldn't enjoy a simple trip to the fair, and I was angry with my son for ruining the highlight of my vacation.

When we got home, I was too worked-up to take the issue up with Jimmy. It was of no use. For the rest of the afternoon, I wallowed in self-pity. That evening, Jim called from New Jersey. He had been with us for part for the trip but his business required that he leave early. He immediately sensed that I was upset and asked me what was the problem.

'It's Jimmy,' I said angrily. 'He had a lulu of a meltdown at the fair today and we all had to come home early. He ruined the day for us.'

'Ah, hon, I'm sorry,' he said. 'But it's more than that isn't it?'

'Well… yes,' I said, my emotions getting the better of me. The line was quiet as I struggled to compose myself.

'Tell me,' urged Jim softly.

'I am so angry,' I wailed quietly. 'I am angry at my son because he ruined my trip. I have been looking forward to seeing all those things for such a long time and now it's over!'

'I'm so sad that things have to be like this.' I was really starting to snivel now. 'Why does everything have to be so hard?'

'It's just the life we have with Jimmy,' said Jim. 'We don't know the reasons why we have to struggle with everything.'

'I know,' I sobbed, boo-hooing into the phone line. 'Hey, you are starting to sound like me,' I said laughing through my tears.

'I guess it's my turn to sound like you,' Jim laughed.

'I just wish that we could be a normal family and do all the things that other families can do without ever having to think twice.'

But then, where would the 'adventure' come in? Jim asked, alluding to the advice given on our wedding day. We both laughed. There was no sense in beating this horse to death.

'I'm sorry that I'm crying,' I said sheepishly. 'I don't mean to bring all this on you.'

'Echo, it's OK to cry.'

One thing I've always had to keep in mind when traveling with Jimmy is the need to be very patient with him as he took the time to re-adjust and transition to each new hotel, restaurant or amusement park. One of the things that helps is to let him pack a good amount of items that he needs to make the transition from home to the new place. A few years ago, we drove the car down to Washington D.C. to visit all the historic sites. Jimmy was allowed to bring a box of toys. I'll never forget the sight of him laboring as he pushed the large box of *Toy Story* toys to the elevator in the parking garage, through the hotel lobby and up to our room. All the characters from the movie made the trip, and Jimmy was all the more comfortable, even if he rarely touched the toys while on the trip. Just knowing that they are there is help enough.

Over the years, I have just resigned myself to supervising Jimmy when we go to trips to the amusement park. Such places are often crowded, noisy, and an orgy of overstimulation. Often Jimmy will take at least the better part of an hour to get used to the place. He won't enjoy any of the rides until he is first comfortable with his surroundings. This can be problematic if I am the only adult with both the kids. Poor Caroline would want to go on a wild amusement ride and I would have to tell her to wait. She was too small to go off by herself. When my husband makes the trip, he will take her off to do as they please; Jimmy and I will enjoy the park in a more sedate fashion. My life with my son is roller-coaster enough in and of itself, I don't feel as though I'm missing out on any kind of fun in not going on all the rides a park has to offer.

The stress is not over once we return from a vacation holiday. Often times, we would find that it would take Jimmy several weeks to re-adjust to the flow of life at school after a lengthy vacation. In the early years, this concerned us, but we now realize that this is just a part of who Jimmy is. There is nothing we can do but 'go with the flow'. When we accepted this as a constant, it made our lives in general a little less stressful. We can't fight what we can't change, only accept the terms of the bargain and work from there, and never forget that once in a while, it's OK to cry.

16

Of Things Motoric

I don't even recall when it first surfaced. It was so subtle that I perhaps didn't pay attention to it. For some reason, which baffled me, Jimmy began to shake, or flap his hands in an odd sort of way. I first noticed the behavior when he was in third grade. Jimmy would first stare off into space, no doubt thinking about a video or television show. Then he would start making little humming noises with his mouth. Lastly, the hands would start to wiggle frenetically.

The first time I noticed this, I watched in bewildered silence. A sense of total helplessness washes over you at a time like this. All of the motivations for Jimmy's hand wiggling seemed internal, and implied that it was a place I couldn't go with him to fix, or stop it. It was as if he had this primal need to flap his hands. Nothing I could do or say could have any effect. As a parent, I felt as though my son was being taken away for short periods of time by some strange force over which I had no control. Before the hand-flapping incidents began, Jimmy would simply just stare off into space. That was a behavior I could handle. But all the new flapping, which his teachers called 'stimming', was just more than I could bear. The new behavior made my son look more impaired than he really was. In the past, Jimmy would be able to quietly enter a social setting without much notice; now, the mannerisms drew the attention of everyone in the room. People would stare. Some, especially children, would snicker. Was I underestimating the depth of his disability? I felt like I was on a runaway train. And I was even more worried for my son's future than I had been in the past.

When Jimmy was little, there was no way I could break through the barrier with him on the issue of his stimming. He just wouldn't (or couldn't) answer me. As his work with Debbie progressed and his language skills improved, he was more able to converse with me about his feelings. When I asked him why he flapped his hands, he told me that it 'relaxes me'. From my point of view, Jimmy certainly needed a lot of 'relaxing'. He stimmed all the time – especially at mealtimes. Going out to a restaurant only brought a spotlight to the behavior. What I would later realize was that Jimmy's need to stim came as more demands were being placed on him. The more he had to do at school, or the more he had to concentrate on eating with good manners, the more he flapped his hands.

Jimmy was about ten before I tried to modify his hand flapping. I had heard Tony Attwood speak about this at a conference, saying kids like Jimmy really need this physical outlet, and that trying to stop this type of activity may bring out a new, and far worse, behavior. I approached Jimmy with my idea at a Burger King restaurant. We had a weekly jaunt to the local fast food eatery during Caroline's weekly piano lesson. Somewhere I had heard the advice that the highest quality parent/child conversation happens at a fast-food restaurant. They called it 'McDonald's Therapy. Want to find out what's on your kid's mind? Take him out for a "Happy Meal."' This approach worked well with my son. I looked forward to my weekly runs to the Burger King with Jimmy as much as he did.

'I want to talk to you about all this hand-waving,' I said as Jimmy was waving furiously. His meal that night had one of his favorite cartoon characters as the 'prize'. Trying to break through the distraction of my son's favorite TV show was a tough job. Jimmy's 'whoop-whooping' was turning the heads of the other restaurant patrons.

'You know when you do this thing with your hands – you know, the thing that relaxes you,' I said demonstrating Jimmy's unique flapping technique. 'Well, I have to tell you something. When you do this, it makes people stare at you.'

'I don't want people to stare at me,' Jimmy said. He had stopped playing with the toy and began pulling the pickle pieces out of his cheeseburger. I swear if the cook held off the pickle, Jimmy would feel cheated out of the ritual.

'Do they laugh at me?' Jimmy asked.

'Well, the grownups don't but some of the kids do,' I said honestly. After my Santa experience, I vowed never to lie again.

'What do I do so they won't?' Jimmy said, looking around the restaurant to see if anyone was still staring at him.

'Well let's think about it,' I said with a plan already in place in my mind. 'What happens at school? Do you flap your hands at school?'

'Uh huh.'

'I think that it makes the kids stare when you do it at school, don't you?'

'I don't want to kids to look at me,' Jimmy reiterated.

'Well how about this,' I said. 'Why don't you try to keep your hands still when you are with your friends at school. When you come home, you can do it all you want. When we go out to a restaurant, I will help you remember, OK?' Jimmy and I then made an agreement that I would gently place my hand on his knee under a restaurant table if he needed a reminder when we were out eating.

The strategy seemed to work, although it wasn't as effective in the beginning. The goal in my mind was for Jimmy to be able to differentiate the social situations where stimming was, and was not, appropriate. It seemed as though I was always giving him a gentle reminder. I wondered if he was ever going to be able to learn this.

About a year later something happened which let me know that Jimmy had indeed internalized this strategy. He had invited a classmate to the house for an overnight sleepover. It was a huge event for our whole family. Jimmy had never been invited to anyone's house to sleep, and at age eleven, he had finally mustered up the courage to have his classmate over.

The evening went well. The young boy who came to the house was simply a delight, had known Jimmy for three years, and appreciated his quirks. When Jimmy became overloaded and retreated to his bedroom, his friend simply sought me out in the kitchen. We ended up baking a fancy chocolate cake. Jimmy came back to help us make the chocolate curls that festooned the top of the cake. The boys were so proud of their 'chef' experience. They insisted that I take a photo, which they later took to their speech class to show Debbie. To my relief, the sleepover was a success!

After we dropped off Jimmy's classmate at his home, I noticed in the car on the ride back that Jimmy was stimming vigorously. 'Whoa!' I thought to myself. 'What's going on here?! He was so good the whole time his friend was here...' And that was when it dawned on me. Jimmy had largely been able to contain his urge to stim while his friend was visiting. Now that it was 'safe', he was going to let it all hang out. We pulled into the driveway where my husband was performing his Saturday ritual of washing the car. Stimming all the way, Jimmy went into the house and headed straight for his room. I was sure he was mentally exhausted.

'What's with Jimmy?' asked Jim.

'He's flapping all over the place,' I said. 'But don't worry, I see this as a good thing.' I then pointed out that this was the first time I saw Jimmy restrain his impulse to flap his hands. 'As soon as we pulled away from the curb, the hands started going,' I reported. I left my husband to think over this development with his bucket and wash rag and went back into the house happy. Knowing that Jimmy had just begun to develop the skill to comport himself in public was a huge load off my mind.

Motor issues are often a difficulty for kids with Asperger Syndrome. It is listed as an associated feature in the *DSM-IV*. Parents that I've talked to nearly always tell me that their child is impacted in some way by sub par motor skills. Jimmy is no exception. Ever since he was a baby, we would literally follow him as he walked around the house. It seemed as though I got nothing done in the way of housework. We survived our repeated trips to the hospital emergency room for stitches. When I read how kids with Asperger tend to have an unusual style of walking, all the troubles we had early on started to make sense.

When Jimmy was young, he had difficulties dressing himself. Deanie worked with me to help him gain some skills with putting on his shirts, socks and pants. Up to that point, I had been dressing Jimmy. She said that I had to stop. At age five, he was too old. I was startled. I thought all mothers did this. Jimmy was my first child, what did I know?

Deanie had suggested that I record my own cassette tape that broke down all the components of the dressing and personal hygiene for Jimmy. I had heard there were some professionally done recordings already in the marketplace, but I couldn't find them. I had the sense that the idea was worthy, but Jimmy would not respond to my voice coming out of a tape recorder. So I did what I thought made sense at the time. I started singing.

Call me wacky, but every morning I would follow my son around the house as he got ready for school with a song on my lips. As I observed, I would just compose the appropriate lyrics to go along with the need of the moment. I always borrowed tunes that many times just popped into my head. One favorite was, 'You Gotta Go Pee...' which I sung to the tune, *I Gotta Be Me*. All the lyrics were impromptu. Later, Caroline would compare me to the American comedienne Rosie O'Donnell, who often sings her own lyrics to well-known tunes on her TV talk show. Both my kids seemed to respond to my singing. I would sing, 'Pick It Up, Pick It Up, Pick It Up-Up-Up...' to the *William Tell Overture* if I was in the room cleaning mode. Or 'Brush Your Teeth, Brush Your Teeth, Brush Your Teeth-Teeth-Teeth...' if we were in the bathroom. I stole from Gershwin's *Fascinating Rhythm* ('Now you put your pants on...

ta-da-da-duh-da'). No composer was immune. Whatever tune popped in my head was good enough. The lyrics just flowed from my head on the spot. Later, I learned the professionals would call this strategy 'cueing'. I just thought I was being a desperate mom doing what came instinctively, hoping my kids didn't sing some of my gems to the other kids at school.

At age nine, after the Asperger Syndrome diagnosis, Jimmy could still not tie his shoes. I was very upset by this. I had tried everything that I could to get him to tie his shoes. Nothing seemed to work. I invested in videos, books, and pretend shoes with big laces. Caroline even sat down for a shoe-tying lesson with Jimmy. No success. It was getting to the point where I was berating Jimmy for being lazy and not trying. Emotion had crept into the scheme of things. I wanted him to do it so badly – Jimmy wasn't going to do it.

I had gone to a meeting with Jimmy's school team. I had pointed out that the doctors who diagnosed Jimmy had recommended that he get some help with life skills such as shoe tying, dialing the telephone, telling time, and handling money. I fully expected to be denied services. Other parents in the United States with whom I had communicated with via e-mail had all pretty much said the same thing: Jimmy needed occupational therapy and if I thought the schools were going to help, I was dreaming.

It just didn't make sense to me. This was a life skill. Didn't the educational law in my country cover the teaching of life skills? I spoke with the school psychologist, who was a member of the team. I pointed out that Jimmy was going to middle school very soon and he would need to have the skills in order to change into his gym clothes. She agreed with me and successfully used the gym class rationale to lobby for occupational therapy services.

After much paperwork, red tape and evaluation rigmarole, Jimmy was assigned Mrs. B., a lovely young occupational therapist. Before she began her work with Jim, she rang me up to see what I thought Jimmy's greatest needs were. 'If you can teach this child how to tie his shoes, I'll be forever in your debt,' I said. 'He's a stubborn old mule.'

Two days later, Jimmy came bashing into the house after his ride home on the school bus. 'Mom! Mom!' he said as excitedly as I had ever witnessed. 'I learned how to tie my shoes!'

'That's wonderful!' I gushed. 'Would you like to show me?'

Jimmy looked down at his own shoes. They had Velcro closures. He frowned and started to look around the room.

'How about me?' I asked, extending my sneakered foot forward.

With a clunk as his backpack was slipped off his shoulders and fell to the floor, Jimmy bent down to tie my shoe. It was the most sublime foot experience since Cinderella got her glass pump returned by the prince. I knelt down and Jimmy embraced me. He was clearly pleased, which was a rare thing for my son, who was often so lacking in emotion. My eyes became moist with pride. I silently thanked Mrs. B. for her wizardry. It had only taken her two sessions to teach my son what I had been trying to do for four years – then again, she's the professional. If I had not taught Caroline to tie her shoes two years earlier, I would have felt like a total wash out as a mother.

'Tell you what,' I said. 'How about we go to the sneaker store and let you pick out any pair of shoes you want. Would you like that?'

'Can I show Daddy?' Jimmy asked.

'You bet!' I said. 'Would you like to show him on your own brand new sneakers?' The deal was made. For the first and only time in his life, Jimmy would look forward to getting a new pair of shoes. I only hoped that he wouldn't pick out the $100 pair of Nike Air Jordan's. But you know what? If he did, I would have bought them anyway. The occasion demanded it.

Another area where Jimmy was a 'late bloomer' was bike riding. Rather than getting professional help from an occupational therapist, we have to credit Caroline with motivating Jimmy to get off the dime and learn to ride his two-wheeled bike without the training wheels. In many cases with Jimmy, there is no better inducement to try a new skill than good old-fashioned sibling rivalry.

When Caroline turned five, Jim and I bought her a brand new bike. After a few months of riding with the training wheels on, she announced to my husband that she was ready to learn to ride with just two wheels. He willingly obliged, getting out his crescent wrench to take off the training wheels. The two spent an afternoon getting the hang of riding on two wheels, with Jim getting the workout of his life, running behind his daughter's bike. After a while, they decided to practice on the grass in the backyard. If she fell, it would be less painful or serious than if she did on the pavement. So in circles they went, with Jimmy and I watching nearby. All the while, Jimmy was agitating about how dangerous it was for his sister to be riding her bike without her training wheels. Like the ice-skating incident, safety issues were preoccupying his mind. After a few minutes on the grass, Caroline finally caught on, and was riding her bike by herself.

Jim and I were thrilled with her accomplishment. The grin on our daughter's face was one of those snapshot moments that every mother carries in her heart forever. We applauded from the sidelines of our backyard and focused our attentions on encouraging her to keep trying. Jimmy, on the other hand, was not pleased at all. He began to act strangely. At first he walked out in front of Caroline's path. She would just steer around him. Then he tried to reach out and grab at her as she rode past. Jim and I got him to move away. 'We don't want anyone to get hurt,' we called. But Jimmy was obsessed. He ran behind a tree and picked up a small limb that had blown to the ground. He ran up to his sister and thrust the stick into the spokes of her bike wheels, bringing her to the ground. Jim and I were horrified.

After determining that Caroline was uninjured, Jim motioned for me to handle the situation with Jimmy. He was too angry with his son to deal with him effectively. We had learned that raving at him at the top of our lungs did no good. Jimmy responded to, and modified his behavior only when we discussed things calmly and rationally, which was often nearly impossible when you wanted to send your kid to the moon. Most mothers had to collect themselves by taking a deep breath and counting to 100. Not me. I had to count to 1,000. At times like this, I was the designated disciplinarian. I marched Jimmy off to his room and as calmly as I could, gave him a lecture within an inch of his life. He offered no explanation as to why he tried to hurt his sister. In my mind, the old safety obsession didn't hold in this case, there was something more. Jimmy wouldn't hurt his sister just to keep her from being hurt. It didn't make sense. Jimmy was too logical a thinker to go about the issue that way. There was something more.

I banished Jimmy to his room and left to go back outside. As I left the house, I could hear him throwing his toys against the wall. Such a physical response was so rare. I re-joined Jim and Caroline out in the backyard. 'He's madder than a wet hen,' I said to Jim. 'I don't know what's up, but I'm sure we'll find out in due time.'

It didn't take long. For the rest of the morning, Jimmy watched us from the window in his bedroom. He was glowering. 'I guess that his sister has insulted his manhood,' I whispered sardonically to my husband, who was mildly amused at his son's behavior. At lunch, we sat down to eat in the kitchen and Jimmy announced at the end of the meal that he would like to learn to ride without his training wheels. Jim and I held in our laughter. In two hours' time, Jimmy had made the emotional transition to a two-wheeled bike. That day, Jim and I learned the value of a little friendly sibling 'leadership'. It would serve us well. In many other instances, it would be Caroline leading the way for her brother. It will be a role that she will have for life, perhaps long after Jim and I are gone.

Time has a way of creeping up on you. All mothers know the experience that our babies don't stay small forever. There comes a time when we must let our children spread their wings and fly solo.

As the mother of a son with Asperger Syndrome, this is a difficult thing. I have spent so much of my time shepherding him through life, helping him interpret his environment. How do I know when the right time comes? If I make a mistake and push too soon, the consequences are long lasting. Parents of typical children could muse the same, but for me, the details of everything concerning my son have to be considered: the noise level of the room, the context of his statements, whether we can take a normal walk in the park without running into someone's dog. All these seemingly tiny matters require constant thought, and is mentally exhausting for a parent to keep current on everything. As Jimmy approaches adolescence, my fears have become heightened. A recent trip to a large store was a huge reality check for me, and has caused me to wonder how well Jimmy will manage on his own in the future.

At times, Jimmy walks with an unusual gait. He takes tiny steps and will hold his torso very stiffly. He won't swing his arms in a natural fashion. This is especially visible when Jimmy feels that he is being watched. Recently, I had taken both children to a store to shop for Easter things. As is my custom, I let the kids do their own looking around, but stay very close. When they were young, I never let them out of my sight, but Jimmy was 12 and needed some autonomy. Knowing that he is a very cautious child, I had recently allowed him a little more space to roam during our shopping trips.

Jimmy had spotted an item that he was very interested in. He had pointed it out to me and I said we had to discuss the purchase first. We had walked several yards away before agreeing that he would buy the item. I sent him back to fetch it. As I watched, Jimmy shuffled over to the rack where the items were located, which was near the store entrance. As Jimmy scanned the racks for the one that he wanted to buy, I noticed that my son had drawn the attention of a store employee, who obviously was regarding him with suspicion. Jimmy picked up the item that he wanted and tucked it under his arm and shielded it with his chest. From my point of view, he was being very protective of his selection, but from the perspective of the store employee, Jimmy was preparing to shoplift. As Jimmy walked towards me, I saw the man follow him. As Jimmy got closer, he held out the item that he wanted to buy. The employee looked at me questioningly as if to say, 'Is he with you?' I nodded.

The whole incident was non-verbal. Everyone was communicating without words. Jimmy looked like a shoplifter; the employee who was about ready to detain my son was only stopped with a 'look' from me. How do I protect my son from this happening to him in the future? I won't always be there to ward off suspicious store clerks. How can my son ever learn the nuances required to not appear like a shoplifter? I have heard of individuals with Asperger getting in trouble with the authorities because of misunderstandings like these. The irony! The very characteristics of this disability are the same things that raise the hair on the backs of the necks of store security personnel and law enforcement. They look for lack of eye contact, the stiff walking style – all of these features can be viewed as suspicious behavior.

As a mother, the thought of my son being detained by the authorities because of suspicious behavior is a scary reality. As I continue to teach my son as he advances into his teen and adult years, I must turn from the basics like tying one's shoes to more subtle things like how to act natural in a store. If my son is to survive, I must. But how? To ensure Jimmy's life is without incident, I must even change the very way that he walks! Parents of typical children don't give a thought to the way their child walks. Yet I am forced to. I'm no physiotherapist! I'm a mother. A mother who often looks with envy at others who don't have to give a second thought to the little details of their children's lives.

17

My Girly

My daughter turned ten today. I greet the day with mixed emotions. Part of me is so proud of the way she's grown into a lovely young girl, full of life and optimistic about her future. The other part of me cringes at the thought that now I have two kids whose ages are in the double digits, which means that I am on the cusp of turning 40 myself – a prospect that I hear is a day hardly worth celebrating.

I often think about my daughter and how her brother's disability affects her. It is a constant source of worry for me. It can't be an easy thing to grow up the sibling of a child with Asperger Syndrome. Coming from a typical household, I have no point of reference as to how to approach her on her feelings regarding this, and neither does her father. Caroline doesn't talk about her thoughts about her brother very much, but when it happens, she is very candid and articulate. My daughter is the kind of person who keeps her innermost feelings to herself so I value every small opening she offers up. But still I wonder. How much does she keep inside? How many opportunities have I missed because I was too focused on her brother's needs? I do the best I can to meet her needs, but I still get the feeling that she deserves more attention.

Some days, I feel that I am in a 'lose/lose' situation. If I give Jimmy all the attention he requires, Caroline is shortchanged. If I give Caroline the attention she deserves, Jimmy starts to slip. Then there is the attention that I want to give my husband. When is it his turn? What time is left for that? It has been a constant juggling act for me. My husband simply calls me, 'Tired Spice.'

Caroline was born when I was thirty. My pregnancy was uneventful. She was a rowdy, kicky, baby inside the womb. Such wiggle, wiggle, wiggle! The day before I went into labor, the obstetrician who performed an ultrasound said, 'Your "silly baby" has managed to get itself up-side-down inside there.' We hoped that things would 'turn around' before the onset of labor, but they didn't. I ended up having an emergency Caesarian section just to get her out.

Jim was there with the delivery team. He cried when he saw his new daughter. While I was being stitched up, Jim called his parents and announced, 'Our Girly is here.' Ever since then the nickname stuck. Within the family, we've always called Caroline 'Girly'.

After things calmed down at the hospital and I got to hold my new daughter in a quiet place, she smiled at me. I was taken aback. Her brother made we wait four months before his first smile. Ever since the first day, it seemed that everything was so effortless with Caroline. She was such an easy baby to 'read', as opposed to her brother. I could even distinguish between Caroline's cries. There was the 'I'm tired' cry, the 'I'm hungry' cry, and the 'change my diapers right now' cry. Life with this new baby was such a breeze compared to the constant confusion and inadequacy I felt trying to care for her brother. In the beginning, I just chalked my success up to experience. Later, I would feel differently when I realized why her brother *was* such a difficult baby.

We did everything the childcare experts told us to do to prepare Jimmy for the arrival of his new sister. We bought all the books and videos. Even extended family members brought him gifts and took special care of him when they came to visit. Jimmy still wasn't happy. We didn't know it at the time, but his world had just been changed irreparably, which as we would later come to learn, would go against his very nature.

When we arrived home from the hospital, Jimmy seemed fine until the novelty of having a new sister wore off. Even worse, was my trip back to the hospital, just two short weeks after I delivered Caroline, to have an emergency gall bladder removal. Now both my children were without their mother. This was particularly difficult for Jimmy, who may have felt that somehow his new sister was to blame for Mommy going back into the hospital. After his experience with his grandfather, who went to the hospital to die, in hindsight, perhaps he was more anxious than he let on. Being only a two-year-old, he didn't have the language abilities to tell us what was on his mind at the time. Later, he would tell us that people only went to hospitals to have babies or die. Perhaps this would be a clue as to why this event was such a life-altering trigger for Jimmy. I often wonder about the way things happened surrounding Caroline's birth, the gall-bladder surgery, and Jimmy's reaction to the whole course of events. It wasn't the Hallmark Card scenario one sees in the television commercials.

'Take this baby back to the "hosta-bull",' Jimmy demanded when Caroline was four weeks old. With all the information I had read in the sibling preparation classes, I was pretty much expecting Jimmy's remark. It is common for all kids to feel this way when a new baby invades the house. I responded with the suggested answers about how they'll be good friends when she is older, and how his feelings will change in time.

For most parents, this animosity goes away. In our case, I am still hearing, 'I wish Girly never came to live here,' even a decade later. I wonder how much of this is typical sibling rivalry. After all, I remember thinking my kid sister was a pest. The same went for my husband and his little sister. When Jimmy was seven, we would endlessly explain to him that his feelings of jealousy were part of growing up, and that he needed to talk to Mommy when he started feeling these feelings. It was a successful strategy. Anger and jealousy are real feelings and Jimmy was only just learning how to demonstrate them appropriately. The 'Phooey', that Deanie had taught him was wearing thin, and Jimmy needed something more to express anger. He knew that he had some dark feelings inside but there were no labels for him to attach to them. Both Jim and I helped Jimmy to recognize these feelings and appropriately vent his frustrations – verbally rather than physically.

I think about the effect all this has had on Caroline. She couldn't help but overhear the many discussions we had with Jimmy about his feelings for his sister. How much of an impact has it had on her? I took great precautions to spend a good deal of one-on-one quality time with her after these flare-ups with Jimmy occurred. I felt it a necessity to reinforce the difficulties her brother was having. His feelings were normal. All kids have them about their brothers and sisters. It was just that in our family's case, the feelings had to be discussed in minute detail so her brother could make sense of it all. What should have been a normal affirmation of love and understanding between a mother and daughter was always overshadowed by her brother's presence and needs.

I tried to come up with different ways to make Caroline feel special. One time, I was running errands in the car with the children when I told Caroline she was my 'Sunshine Girl' because she always smiled so much. Seemed so simple at the time. Yet of course it was more complicated.

'What about me?' Jimmy asked from the passenger's side front seat. To this day, he always sits in the same seat in the front of the car. Caroline must sit in the back. There is no room for discussion. Other families' kids fight over taking turns to sit in the front seat. Not our family. It's set in concrete. Jimmy always gets the front. Sure, it's not fair. But Caroline realized that sitting in the back was far better than having a huge argument and the car window broken by her brother.

'What about me? What kind of a boy am I?' Jimmy prompted. My mind immediately went to the *Peanuts* cartoon character 'Pig Pen', who is always followed by a dust cloud. In my son's case, I visualized a little rain cloud. His expression and demeanor is so dour and serious all the time.

'You, my darling son, are my little rain cloud,' I announced happily. As soon as the words escaped my lips, I knew there would be trouble. Jimmy wouldn't understand my figurative language. I braced myself for the barrage.

'I'm a cloudy boy? That's bad.' I looked at his sweet face. It was crestfallen. How could I be so stupid!

'You are not a bad boy!' I said emphatically. 'You are a good boy!'

'But you just said I was a rain cloud and Girly was a sunshine.'

'That's right, Jimmy. I did say that.' My mind was racing. How could I bail myself out of this pickle I had gotten myself into? I hated the thought of hurting my child's feelings. Why can't anything be simple! How does it happen that everything turns out to be about Jimmy?

'A little grumpy, stormy, rain cloud…' Jimmy said sarcastically.

'Now let's think,' I said calmly. 'Every thing needs sun to grow, but the rain clouds are just as important. I enjoy all of Girly's smiles just like a sunny day. But think, Jimmy. We all need water too to grow. You and I like to go sit out on our porch and listen to the rain come down, right?'

Jimmy nodded. He had come out on a couple of occasions to join me during those quiet times.

'So if you think about it, I enjoy both of my two kids in very much the same way that I enjoy sun and rainy days.'

'So I'm your rainy day?'

'Yes, son.'

'And I'm your sunny girl?' asked Caroline.

'Yep! And I need both of you equally. It just wouldn't be an interesting life if you kids were both the same.' To my relief, the explanation seemed to satisfy Jimmy. Yet I was bothered. Why couldn't I just be able to freely pay my daughter a compliment without it having to escalate into a federal case with her brother. Why must everything be so complicated all the time?

If Caroline was involved, everything was a big deal to her brother. There were some days when I felt that he was just stomping the life out of her with his words. One of the things Caroline likes to do is sing freely when the urge arises. She gets it from her mother. I've tried to foster the habit in both my children, however unsuccessfully with Jimmy. If mother sings, that's OK. Jimmy will have second thoughts about telling his mother to shut up. When a sister does it, siblings have no qualms about telling each other what's on their mind. And for years, Jimmy's thoughts were obsessed with telling his sister to be quiet.

She was a constant source of distraction and irritation to him. When he was trying to do his homework in elementary school, we had to have the house totally silent or Jimmy would become disengaged and his stream of concentration would be broken. Usually, Caroline would be the culprit and Jimmy would fuss at her. Then I would raise my voice to her because I had worked with Jimmy on his homework papers and I must start the process over. It just wasn't a good situation. My child had to keep silent in her own house? Not only was this unfair, but impossible! Caroline couldn't bring her friends in because they would make too much noise and bother her brother's concentration. At the time, I had no solution to this dilemma. We lived with this for several years until thankfully, Jimmy was able to tolerate more background noise as he got older. I can't help but worry and wonder if this had any lasting impact on my daughter.

There were some times when Jimmy wouldn't even allow Caroline to talk. He was constantly telling her to be quiet. It was as though the sound of her voice was like fingernails on a chalkboard. After his diagnosis of Asperger Syndrome, I could understand why his sister's high-pitched voice might bother Jimmy's sensitive ears. But do I allow the silence of one child simply for the comfort of another? I didn't care if Jimmy had a disability, he was going to have to get used to the sound of his sister's voice or go to another room.

'It's just not fair,' wailed Caroline, after a particularly grueling argument with her brother. I had to intervene and separate the two children. Each had drawn time out in their respective bedrooms.

'I'm sorry,' I told my sobbing daughter. ' I don't like it either, and I really don't know what to do about Jimmy.'

'I hope I never have an Asperger boy,' said Caroline with contempt. 'All they do is want things their own way and hurt your feelings.'

My daughter's words sliced through me. The thought of never having Jimmy in my life, or an altered Jimmy, a de-Aspergered Jimmy just seemed so cold and foreign to me. Truth be told, there is a very good chance that my daughter would have an 'Asperger boy'. Scientific research has given strong credence to the genetic link of families with children who have autistic spectrum disorders. Caroline could very well follow the same path as a mother that I have.

'Chickie,' I said, holding her on my lap. 'I know… it's hard being the Mom of an "Asperger boy". But Heavenly Father might decide to give you one to raise. And if He does, you will be a prepared Mommy for that boy because you learned about Asperger from living with Jimmy.'

'I really don't want one,' she whimpered, wiping her runny nose on my shirt, her tears starting to wane. 'Is it OK if I am just an Asperger teacher?'

I laughed. This was during the time in her life when Caroline's life wish was to grow up and become a schoolteacher. 'Of course! That sounds like a good idea. I bet you'll be the best Asperger teacher ever!'

There are some that say that I shouldn't worry so much. I remember chatting with a friend, another writer, who wanted me to look over her manuscript for a children's book she was writing. She was very familiar with Caroline and adored her. We started talking about my concerns about her happiness. One of the things she confided to me was that she was the sibling of a Down's Syndrome child.

'I want you to know that I saw my mother worry,' she said of her large family. 'As much as she tried to hide it from us, we could see it every time we looked at her. For Caroline's sake, don't worry so much.'

I thought about what she had said. How do you avoid the appearance of worry? True, kids can smell a mother's worry, however subtle. I saw my aunt worry about her third child, a son who was born with a severe heart condition. The family lived through some horrific medical dramas, particularly in the teen years. But I was around enough to be able to perceive my aunt's constant distraction. Her worry was always there. It never left her, just as my worry about Jimmy will never leave me. It makes me wonder how my daughter must feel. If I recognized it in my cousin's family, surely she feels my distraction.

The best I can do is keep an open dialog with her. There are days when she wishes he were dead. But the next day, she will show him kindness that warms the heart. Jimmy realizes that his sister loves him, and although he is unable to express his love and appreciation to her, he will show little clues that indicate to me that he cares too. One evening, we were riding home from his grandmother's house in the car. It was cold and Caroline had not brought her coat. Jimmy shared his coat with her, keeping her warm until we got to the house, where the warm and fuzzy moment abruptly came to an end when he called her a 'butt-head'. I live for those small shows of kindness. It is remarkable for a child with Asperger to even recognize another's discomfort, much less respond appropriately. All the lessons of kindness I've repeatedly pounded into my kid's heads have somehow taken root. When my kids are kind to each other, it is the supreme 'Mommy-Moment'.

I've taken great effort to carefully explain to Caroline the aspects of her brother's condition. She knows more about how his mind works than he does. There are times when she needs to handle a situation with the neighborhood kids, when a parent would be more intrusive. Jimmy rarely goes outside to play, and when he does make an appearance, it is usually a short one. Then Caroline would have to explain her brother's quick disappearance with, 'He just likes to be alone.'

Caroline also knows that there is a slight possibility that she will be the one to look after her brother after Mommy and Daddy are gone from this earth. We've talked about it openly. I think the reality of Jimmy's situation hit home with her when the two were working on the same homework assignments, and even more when her homework grew increasingly more difficult than his. As an adult, Jimmy may need someone to help him. Or to look in on him from time to time. Caroline's role will be what the two of them define. Together, they'll lay out the ground rules for their relationship. She may be a listening ear, or money manager, or both – only time will tell.

As far as my own relationship with my daughter, I would hope that we grow to enjoy the kind of friendship that I have with my own mother. Doing this will require much continued effort on my part. I cannot assume that everything will be OK with my daughter simply because she seems to function well in society. Like any child, she has her agonies, her ecstasies, and all these must be paid attention to. I must not allow my worry and preoccupation with her brother's disability to overshadow her relationship with me. It's a constant ballet. I feel as though I'm dancing as fast as I can. The teen years are coming Then the tempo picks up. Will we be dancing to the same tune? She's ten today. I only have eight more years before she becomes of age. In the grand scheme of things, that is not long at all. Time has a tendency to pass all too quickly. Before I know it, she'll be gone, my nest emptied of one little 'chickie'. I pray that the only baggage she takes with her is the kind she physically packs in her suitcase – not the emotional kind.

18

Finding His Passion – and Beyond

When Jimmy was ten, Jim and I took him to a shopping mall, where we stopped for lunch in a food court. My husband had gotten us our food, which included the required cheeseburger Happy Meal for Jimmy, which he promptly wolfed down. Our son was getting bigger. Not only was he requiring bigger sizes in clothes, but now, the amount of food in a kid-sized meal was not enough to satisfy his hunger. He asked for another cheeseburger.

My husband gave Jimmy some cash and sent him back up to the counter, where from a distance, we could keep a good eye on how things progressed. At first, Jimmy had a hard time deciding how to stand in the line that had formed. As soon as he would take a spot, his attention would draw elsewhere, and the line would shorten, only Jimmy would not keep up. Other hungry shoppers would take their place in front of our daydreaming son. Jim and I wondered if Jimmy would ever make it to the front of the counter to even place his order.

After several minutes of trial and error, with my husband and I quietly panting, 'You can do it, Jimmy,' from our distant outpost, Jimmy finally made it to the front and ordered his cheeseburger. The attendant took the cash, and after beckoning Jimmy back for his change, turned to fill the order – or so we thought. As our son stood by, the world seemed to pass him by. Customers revolved past him, placing their orders and leaving with food. Our son just stood and waited. After several minutes, it was clear that something had gone wrong. Jim and I, reluctant to give up and intervene, stayed watching from afar, hoping with all our hearts that our son could successfully order a cheeseburger, something that most parents of other ten-year-old boys take for granted.

Finally we had to give in. Clearly, Jimmy was unable to advocate for himself by asking, 'Hey! Where's my cheeseburger!' His language skills and ability to read the social situation was not developed enough for him to make a sound judgement. Jim had to go up to the counter and get the cheeseburger. Our son had waited over five minutes. It was clear to us that his first foray into fast food had gone awry. As parents, we were crushed by the experience. It showed us how much more work we had to do to prepare Jimmy to live an independent adult life.

At that point, Debbie only had two more years to work with our son before he would move on to middle school. She continued to stress social language and how to self-advocate and Jimmy made some huge gains from age ten to age twelve. One day, I was in the kitchen with Jimmy and had asked him a question. I didn't get a response right away, which was common. Before I could ask the question again, Jimmy said, 'I'm sorry Mom. Could you repeat that?' I was delighted. Debbie had obviously made a breakthrough. I couldn't wait to tell her the next time I saw her. Another time, I was in a hurry with Jimmy and peppered him with questions about an upcoming homework assignment. His response showed a maturity that delighted me.

'Slow down Mom! You're asking me too many questions. You're making my brain all confused.'

Most mothers would take offense at this kind of attitude from their children. For me, it was as wonderful as Jimmy learning to walk. Unlike the rabid excitement displayed by both Jim and I the time Jimmy took his first steps at a Fourth of July picnic; this event required that I play the 'Duh Mom' role, lest I be told to 'chill out' in Asperger terms.

Another common sense strategy we found to be very effective is what the professionals call 'Scripting'. I used the technique early on because it made sense and came naturally to me and I am always amused when my research turns up an official-sounding term for my approach.

Scripting gives Jimmy an overview of a social situation, and how the conversation might go. I have given Jimmy scripting for nearly everything from how to order a pizza, to calling up a close family member. Some times it goes well – sometimes it doesn't. It can be very difficult for Jimmy just to dial the telephone. In the beginning it was torturous. Halfway through dialing, he would forget the number. His frustration would boil over and he would hang up the phone in disgust. After months of trial and error, we figured out that he needed to have the phone number on a card. Trying to scan for a number from a list seemed to be a hard thing to do from a visual standpoint. There was just too much on the page for him to try and process from page to telephone keypad. To this day, he still hates to place a phone call. There are too many cognitive steps involved in punching in the number. By the time he gets the number dialed, Jimmy is so rattled that sometimes he forgets who he is calling. Most adolescents take their telephone activity for granted. I think people, even extended family members, have no idea how big of an accomplishment it is for my son to place a simple phone call.

Some ignorant parents and strangers, who have overheard me coaching my son, who is now as tall as my eyebrows, have made such snide comments, such as 'you're putting words in his mouth,' or 'can't he speak for himself?' I let the sting of such thoughtless barbs roll off the best that I can. To even bother to try and explain how far my son has come and what his difficulties are would be a waste of breath.

Scripting came in very handy during an incident when Jimmy had been bullied by a classmate. One evening, I answered the phone and the caller asked for Jimmy. I knew who it was. The boy's distinctive voice was familiar to me because I had spent so much time in Jimmy's classroom as the room mother. During the course of the one-sided conversation, I could tell that Jimmy was becoming confused and agitated. He motioned for me to listen in. I was shocked to hear the other student threaten a beating, and other forms of intimidation. It was out of character for this boy. I wasn't worried that this child would make good on the threats. What worried me more was that my son would be so scared, he would not go to school anymore. After Jimmy reassured his caller that he was sure of his identity, he hung up the phone in a panic. I was inspired to come up with a 'expose the bully' plan.

The next day, I instructed Jimmy. 'When Mrs. C. asks the class what was new (as was her custom), you need to raise your hand and tell the class what happened,' I said. Jimmy gulped hard. Clearly, he was not looking forward to doing this. I scripted it out. Repeatedly, with great detail, I went over what he was to say the next day in class: The boy called. He tried to disguise his voice but did a bad job, 'because I could tell who it was. He told me he was going to beat me up in the playground,' and (most important) 'Isn't that the funniest thing you've ever heard!' I wrote a note outlining my strategy with the teacher and nervously waited until Jimmy came home from school the next day.

The teacher reported back to me that the idea worked – very well. Jimmy raised his hand, told his story and the whole class laughed at the phone antics of their classmate, who slunk low in his desk with total embarrassment. The phone rang later that night and it was the classmate, who identified himself properly to me this time. No more threats were made. If anything, Jimmy held a new respect in the eyes of this boy, who saw that my son would not be cowed.

I have realized over the last several years that life is Jimmy's classroom and there is no summer break. I am forever on the lookout to make some kind of lesson out of the little vignettes that make up our life. Whether it's teaching humor, how to handle money, striking up a conversation. All of these, I've learned, have to be directly taught to kids like Jimmy. He won't ever learn it through osmosis, like his peers do.

One day, I was contemplating how I could get Jimmy to stop picking his nose in public. His teacher had even commented to me that she was trying to get him to use a tissue. I was embarrassed. As I sat in my car with both the kids, I looked around at the other drivers who had stopped at the traffic light. As I glanced in my rearview mirror, I caught one of my fellow drivers in the act of cleaning out his olfactory organ with his pinky finger.

'Don't turn around,' I said calmly to the kids, tapping my finger on my rearview mirror. 'But I want you to look in this mirror and see what the person behind us is doing.'

The kids unbuckled their seatbelts to get a good look. I relished their squeals of disgust as they stated the obvious.

'What an idiot,' said Jimmy. 'He better not eat it!'

'Now you know what it looks like when people watch you pick your nose,' I said, hoping that this impromptu social skills lesson was sinking in.

A couple days later, his teacher pulled me aside and asked, 'Did you take him to a behavioral therapist? He's stopped picking his nose.'

I choked back a laugh. 'Naw,' I said. 'I just took him to Driver's Ed,' thankful that the guy in the car behind me had just saved me a couple of hundred in professional fees.

Another thing I had to develop my patience with, is the fact that the neurologic functioning of Jimmy's brain is different than most of us. It takes Jimmy three times a long to learn a new concept or idea. His teachers need to know that it is imperative that they teach things to him correctly the first time. Because if he learns something wrong, it'll take months to get him to un-learn the wrong thing and re-learn the right thing.

Jimmy enjoys going to yard sales, scouring the piles of old toys for the one unique thing that might have been overlooked. I find that these times alone with him on Saturdays provide a wealth of opportunity. Jimmy has quality time with me, and I script things out for him so that he can practice his conversation skills. He also must make purchases and come up with the proper amount and count his change. I have found that individuals have much more patience for my son on the lawn in front of their house than they would at a place of business. Jimmy has more of an opportunity to strike up a conversation with someone at a yard sale than he would at a retail establishment. Yard sales provide a good forum for him to practice his newly developing skills in a non-threatening arena. My son really enjoys it when we go 'yard sailing'. I remember one time Jimmy found some Happy Meal toys that he missed as part of 'his collection'. We paid pennies for these little toys and you would have thought that he had found the Holy Grail. So when the weather turns nice, we grab the classified advertments and scan the listings for possible sales. If it's a Saturday morning, you'll know Jimmy and I are off mining the yard sales.

One of the things that I work hard to do is give my son a taste of as many different things that interest him as possible. One day, something will catch fire with him and he will become obsessed enough to become a very skilled and adept person in this area. Right now, he wants to be a toy inventor. Last week, he wanted to be a scientist. The week before that, he wanted to be Mr. Bean. I've encouraged him to explore various different experiences. As a result of a summer golf camp, Jimmy enjoys golf, although you need to grab your hard hat and board up your windows when he hits the ball. He enjoys going to antique shops and has quite a sophisticated taste in old toys. Perhaps he will find an avocation as a dealer in antiques? Or a computer programmer. The possibilities all lie in front of him. My job as his mother is to help him find his passion. To me, this is the key for him to secure employment successfully in his adult life. One day, Jimmy is going to find something that he enjoys, and he'll do it very well, and make a career out of it.

I have spent the first part of Jimmy's life intervening in the area of language acquisition. Thanks to Debbie, Deanie, and all the professionals who have worked with him, Jimmy's made marvelous strides and has grown with huge leaps. As we look ahead, the direction that we need to take is in getting him prepared academically for a challenging future. My beautiful baby has grown into a handsome young man. Peach fuzz now adorns his upper lip, hormones are starting to rage, and he's starting to ask me about girls. Like most boys his age, he's stuck in that hard place that sits between the desire to grow and be autonomous and wanting to be a kid forever. He'll spend a typical day after school playing video games, fussing over his homework, wolfing down his dinner and will then retire to the solitude of his bedroom to read or listen to his music till all hours of the night if we let him. The normality of his behavior pleases me, although watching my son change, especially when change is so difficult for individuals with Asperger Syndrome, is hard, and a hard thing to try and help him cope with. Not only is his life changing, with more classroom pressures and social demands, but his body is physically changing too. Thankfully, Jimmy has gotten much more flexible about dealing with changes in his life. However, there are little things that will still throw him. I still have to patiently explain why he can't go to the pancake house and still order the kid's meal. The rules say that he is too old now. When we go out to eat, the hostess still gives his sister the special placemat and the crayons. Jimmy, a twelve-year-old who is nearly as tall as his mother, is now ignored. 'What about me?' he asks plaintively. 'Where are my crayons?' The disappointment in his face about the little things is what makes me hurt the most.

A highly respected child psychiatrist told me that the most difficult times in the life of a person with Asperger Syndrome are the transitions from elementary school to middle school, and the shift from college to the world of work. This year, Jimmy made the jump from elementary school to middle school. It wasn't an easy year for him, but with the help of a receptive team of professionals at the new school, Jimmy has made it through most of the year. I want him to be happy about the progress that he's made, but for kids like Jimmy, who now insists that I call him Jim, even positive changes are unsettling.

He has the benefit of a full-time teacher's aide, who makes sure that he gets from one class to another, formats all of his curriculum materials in the way that Jimmy needs to learn best, and also provides the constant re-direction of Jimmy's attention to the lessons in class. At times, she also re-teaches the material as necessary. One of the other things that we learned was that the environment in middle school is much more demanding of our son. Getting on the noisy, crowded bus in the morning – waiting for the first bell with a crowd of restless kids on the school's lawn – rushing in the building with the rest of the students once the bell rings – being jostled and bumped – worrying that he might forget his locker combination – or be late to Homeroom – are all daily activities that were overwhelming my son.

All combined, that first hour of his day was mentally exhausting for Jimmy. He began falling asleep in his second class of the day. This required that we place him on a modified daily schedule. Just a one-hour delay in having Jimmy report to school each day was enough of a difference that allowed him to better function and, more importantly, to learn at his new school.

I often muse about Jimmy's future and what role I see myself playing in it. 'You *are* his Annie Sullivan,' once said my husband. In a very real sense, he's right. Throughout this child's life, I've been helping him interpret his environment. I know what my son can and cannot handle. What things will confuse him. What pleases him. Like most mothers, I know my child best. I've been accused of sheltering my son from the challenges of life. I don't know of any mother of a child with AS who hasn't endured these onslaughts. On this I will stand tough: I will not push my son into a situation before he is ready. I am the authority and expert. If my husband defers to me, the rest of the world needs to as well. If we throw our kids into society before they are ready, the consequences may take years of remedy. Mothers, listen to your inner voice. Base your decisions about your child's future on 'mother gut' – not 'mother guilt'. In the long run, your own instincts will serve you – and your child – well.

Jimmy and I have had talks about his moving away from home after he's grown. He's even brought up the subject of marriage. I have every confidence that Jimmy will be capable of a successful marriage. It's a matter of whether he chooses to marry, and of course, finding the right girl.

'Do you think I'll ever get a wife?'

'Yes, but I think that you will have to look a long, long time for the right girl to be your wife,' I said.

'What will she be like? I want her to be like you.'

'Whoever you pick to be your wife should be a very organized person,' I said, scratching my head.

'Like you?'

'NO! Certainly not like me!' I said with mock horror. 'I'm not the organized one. Daddy is.' Jimmy smiled a sly smile that reminded me again of his grandfather.

'How will I know who is the right one,' Jimmy wondered.

'All of us ask that question,' I mused. 'I think the most important thing about who you choose is that she'll be your best friend.'

'Like you?'

'Yes. You will feel happy with her the same way you feel happy and comfortable with me.'

'Do you think she'll like living here?'

I took a breath and stopped short. 'I think your wife would like to have her own house, don't you? Just like Mommy and Daddy moved out of the house where we grew up and started our own.'

Jimmy just sat and thought. Surely I had just thrown a curve into his neatly laid-out plan. Indeed, where would his wife store all her belongings? There just wasn't enough room for her toys in his toy box. What Jimmy didn't understand at his young age, was that perhaps someday, his urge to leave the nest would be stronger than his need for sameness and security.

Those who ask parents if they would take away their child's disability are insensitive. It is not a very fair question is it? Would I take away Jimmy's Asperger Syndrome? I have mixed emotions about this. So much of who my son is, is so closely tied to his disability. If I took *all* of it away, I wouldn't have my son left. Then I would miss him terribly. Would I take away the fear and anxiety? Sure. Would I give him an increased clarity of mind? Sure. Would I give him social skills? Definitely! But there are many lovely things about Jimmy's 'Aspergerish' personality that I find of value.

Take the insistence of sameness. This area has driven me nuts in the past, but things are slowly coming to the point where Jimmy can effectively live with the small things that used to totally derail him. I suspect that as time goes on, with more intervention, he'll become even more adept at managing change. This trait for sameness can be a desirable one. Should Jimmy marry, his future spouse will find a most loyal and true partner for life. He will have an air of predictability that can serve as a stabilizing force in a marriage.

Jimmy's incredible capacity for rote memory is another benefit that I would not change. In our society, we value individuals who possess this skill. I have worked with several people who have built up a knowledge base in their minds in a particular area, who are the historians, or registrars of large, well-known organizations. It's a diagnostic characteristic worth keeping, don't you think?

As he grows and learns, my son is developing a deliciously wicked sense of humor, one that reminds me of his grandfather. After a recent trip to the dentist to get a cavity filled, Jimmy asked me when he was going to start 'farting', since the dentist had 'given him gas'. Where once there were problems with literal interpretation conflicts, now, there is understanding for Jimmy. He not only gets jokes, he will risk telling them, which is something we've worked hard to accomplish. Just yesterday, he dropped a sugar doughnut in the car and grumbled, 'Gravity!' in disgust. I laughed at his 'scientific' joke. We've some a long, long way from the first joke he ever understood enough to repeat:

'Knock, Knock.'

'Who's there?'

'Boo.'

'Boo, Who?'

'You don't have to cry about it.'

The future is bright for my son. Luckily, his difficulties were brought to our attention very early in his life and we were able to get him interventions. He has grown considerably from the confused child who told his speech teacher he was going to jump out of the window and run home to his mother. Jimmy is now an adolescent. His voice has transformed from that of a boy, through the warbly uncertainty of change, and is now the deep, rich sounding voice of his father. As my son enters adolescence, his world will change, along with the rest of his peer group, but with one difference. For Jimmy, the long elusive moments of clarity are coming much more often than they have in the past. He still may struggle just to be on the same level as those around him, and while he may not win every battle, he is absolutely winning the war.

Evidence of this came clearly to me last Christmas. We had all traveled to my parent's home to celebrate the holidays. My brother and his four children were there, as was my sister. It had been years since we had gotten together at holiday time with our families.

The first flakes of Christmas snow started falling as we arrived from the airport. It was the wonderful fluffy, flaky, crunch-beneath-your-feet white stuff that everyone goes ga-ga over. By the next morning, the snow was up to mid-calf high. Jimmy and Caroline went outside to wander in the white powder. My son's desire to venture outside surprised me as he normally hates going out into freezing temperatures. From the window, I watched Jimmy as he helped his sister build a snowman. His blue eyes shone as he marveled at the Rocky Mountain version of snow. The smile on his face was remarkable – especially for a child who had to be taught how to smile only seven short years ago. As he scooped up the powdery snow and let the wind blow it out of his mittened hands, I gazed at his upturned ruddy cheeks and the shock of sandy brown hair that peeked out from beneath my father's old toboggan hat. Yes, his mind was clear today, as clear as the blindingly blue sky above him. For me, this was the best gift of all that Christmas: my son's spontaneous smile and the promise of clear skies for the life ahead.

Afterword

The Politics of it All...

When I first began researching Asperger Syndrome, one of the big questions on everyone's mind was, 'What is the difference between AS and High Functioning Autism?' Several research papers were written on the subject, most notably a 1995 article by Yale University's Ami Klin and Fred Volkmar, *et al.*, who indicated that those with AS who are administered a Weschler Intelligence Test (WISC) are far more likely to have a verbal IQ subtest score that is higher than their performance IQ subtest score, while those with HFA are the opposite – far more likely to have a higher performance than verbal score. They went on to say that those with AS had a neuropsychological profile that was *empirically different* from those with HFA, and suggested that intervention strategies for those with AS should be *different* than for those with HFA. They elaborated by pointing out that the cognitive profile of AS better resembles a disorder known as Nonverbal Learning Disorder (NLD), which has 30-year roots in the field of neuropsychology, and that the educational intervention strategies used for NLD are recommended for the AS student.

I have found that the most helpful information in the area of educational interventions for Jimmy does, in fact, come from the field of neuropsychology, specifically NLD. Still, as with the old HFA/AS debate, I found that there is tremendous controversy over whether AS and NLD have: (1) overlapping symptomology but are unrelated, or (2) whether both groups have NLD with the AS individuals having a 'dash' of something more, or (3) if they are actually the same disorder with differences in presentation.

So, parents now ask what the difference is between a diagnosis of AS and NLD, and they are often left with more questions than answers. This question is still the topic of considerable scientific debate. In his 1995 book, Dr. Bryon Rourke describes Asperger Syndrome as a 'Level 1' Nonverbal Learning Disability. Translated, this means that AS individuals have virtually all of the neuropsychological assets and deficits of NLD – or full-blown NLD. Confusion? You bet!

An NLD diagnosis has its roots in the field of neuropsychology, the study of the brain and how it works. Asperger Syndrome, on the other hand, has its roots in the field of psychiatry/psychology which only looks at behaviors. If you fit the diagnostic criteria, *as perceived by the consulting clinician*, then you get educational or medical services. The level and scope of services depend on two things: the which state you live in, and insurance company you subscribe to. Unfortunately it's all too common to take your child to three different clinicians and get three differing diagnoses. Diagnosing children is an art, not a science; and not all clinicians are created equal. I am personally frustrated by the fact that my son's neurological condition is in essence a label of a psychiatric disorder, which means that thousands of American children with developmental disabilities such as AS and autism, are actually diagnosed under psychiatric guidelines, when their difficulties are caused by neurobiological factors and affect far more than their behavior. My son has a developmental disability, a medical problem; his troubles are not psychiatric! As frustrated as I am, I have to give credit where credit is due. As I alluded earlier, the professionals in the field of medicine failed our family. We spent years on the medical merry-go-round searching for answers that ultimately were found in the field of psychology. If British researcher Lorna Wing hadn't resurrected Hans Asperger's original paper in her 1981 *Psychological Medicine* article, where would we all be today?

To further complicate the situation, since there are no objective measures used within the field of psychiatry/psychology to diagnose Asperger Syndrome, a diagnosis depends on a clinician's subjective observations. What's in a name? Plenty! I've heard of parents who have taken their child to a psychologist and received a diagnosis of Asperger Syndrome; their neuropsychologist diagnosed NLD; the occupational therapist gave the same child a diagnosis of Sensory Integration Disorder; the Speech Pathologist says it's Semantic-Pragmatic Disorder; and the pediatrician originally thought it was Attention Deficit Disorder.

From an intervention perspective, the discovery of NLD was manna from heaven. The majority of published material on AS interventions were limited to behaviors or social deficits. Within the autism community, interventions did address educational needs but did not seem appropriate for Jimmy. Autism interventions are either visual or multi-sensory, whereas my son is a stronger auditory learner. What we have also found is that Jimmy is a uni-modal learner; that is, he uses one sensory strategy at a time. He cannot 'look' and 'listen' at the same time. Often, teachers will tell me that Jimmy does not appear to be listening or paying attention in class, yet he will know all the material that was discussed. Taking class notes is impossible because it requires two modalities. The majority of the time he learns best through auditory means, other times visual. In our experience, the multi-dimensional strategies tended to overwhelm Jimmy. He would quickly slip into sensory overload.

The NLD community uses a far more comprehensive approach to intervention. Rather than dealing strictly with behaviors, the research deals with the social, the emotional, the academic, the motoric, *and* the environmental areas, providing far more depth. Since this a more comprehensive approach, it stands to reason that there are fewer behavioral issues because *all* the child's issues are being dealt with – not just the interactional component. In my opinion, this is *the* exact program the AS student needs. The NLD literature is attuned to the significant transition periods in their lives

– particularly adolescence. There is a wealth of NLD material, most notably the work of Jean Foss, Sue Thompson, Byron Rourke, Kathy Allen and several others. All of these are excellent starting points in developing an appropriate comprehensive intervention program.

Early recognition and intervention is the key to giving those with Asperger Syndrome their best shot at productive lives. There has been some great work by Dr. Stanley Greenspan in the area of early intervention. Pioneer of the 'Floor-time' play therapy, his methods are targeted for the very young, primarily preschool-age children. In hindsight, the critical factor in helping Jimmy get as far along as he has was the early work of Deanie and Debbie. We were most fortunate to be able to start intense social skills teaching and language-based learning when he was a five-year-old.

As most parents already know, most medical insurance companies do not cover these early interventions. The insurers say that such treatments have no significant impact for long-term independent living. Nothing could be further from the truth! For kids with Asperger Syndrome, the return on even the smallest investment can potentially benefit the whole of society in ways that will boggle the mind.

Government funding for studies and treatment of AS is woefully inadequate. The insurance companies won't pay for services that are critically needed, saying, 'Let the schools handle it.' Strapped school systems are pressuring parents to try their insurance companies first for services. With the 1994 introduction of Asperger Syndrome in the *DSM-IV*, the numbers of individuals who have been diagnosed has grown exponentially. A March 1999 report on Autism to the California State Legislature noted a whopping 1,975-per cent increase in 'Class 4' developmental disabilities (including Asperger Syndrome) during an 11-year period. This was overshadowed by the publicity generated by the report's numbers on autism – an astonishing 272-per cent rise during the same time period. Hopefully, reports such as these are a wake up call to the governments of the world. Whether this sharp increase is due to better recognition of the disorder, or to statistics keeping is open to debate, but the numbers are staggering.

The 'sleeping giant' is beginning to awaken. Schools are being overwhelmed by the sheer numbers of Asperger Syndrome cases, and they are puzzled as to how to best handle these students. Public monies need to be targeted for the research and development of comprehensive intervention programs. This is not a small need. The current prevalence numbers put the incidence of individuals with Asperger Syndrome at 1 in 300. A huge population that is grossly under-served! Furthermore, if you include individuals with similar symptomology, both diagnosed (e.g., NLD, PDD-NOS, Semantic-Pragmatic Disorder) *and* undiagnosed, the numbers of affected individuals would skyrocket! It's going to take a lot of money to address this pressing social need.

Those of us in the Asperger community need to learn from the stellar example set by the autism community and let our friends in government, medicine, and industry know about these issues and help shake loose some resources to address the needs of those who live with this 'hidden' disability. The efforts of the autism community have been so effective that Pervasive Developmental Disorders as a category (as defined in the *DSM-IV*) are more often referred to as 'autistic spectrum disorders'.

Our kids are often the deep thinkers: the Albert Einsteins of this world. With proper intervention, kids like Jimmy can grow to be contributing members of society in ways that can have a huge impact. The future researcher obsessed with finding a cure for cancer may be the AS student of today. If we as parents can teach others to look deeper, to recognize, appreciate, and, if needed, assist with the needs of those with Asperger Syndrome, we will not only make the world a better place for our own children, but perhaps our grandchildren as well. After 50 years, we now have an official diagnosis for this disorder that was first characterized by Hans Asperger. Let's not wait another 50 years for the scientific community to play catch-up. Parents need to advocate publicly for their children to the fullest extent of their capacity. Our kids can't afford to wait for science, and educational innovation to come to them, parents need to seek out the best strategies for their kids, and encourage researchers and educators to look further into the difficulties associated with this disorder. Our kids are told their accomplishments are only limited by their dreams. The same goes for parents. In my conversations with my son, there is the expectation that he will go to college, find a job, live independently, marry and be a father. It is a dream that we jointly share with Jimmy. Our expectations are high, which we must temper with the philosophy that Jimmy's accomplishments will always be met with our enthusiasm and happiness. Our ultimate goal is for our son to grow up to be a happy person who is comfortable living inside his skin. We should never be afraid to dream for our kids. Their success will only be limited by our vision of their future.

All children are like seeds. If you plant them in the ground on the same day, give them all equal amounts of sun and water, you'll find that their individual inner clocks determine when their developmental milestones germinate. Kids with Asperger Syndrome are the late bloomers of this world. They require more sun, more water, and a lot of extra talking to. Their blooms are just as beautiful as any other in the garden, if anything, more unique, with colors far more intense than the norm. We as a society must nurture these children. They are the extraordinary individuals whose contributions to the garden of mankind provide the texture and contrast that are highly sought after in all well tended horticultural patches. Like a globe thistle, our kids first emerge with prickly burrs that must be cultivated before we can enjoy their unique and beautiful blooms. As parents and as a society, we must give them the means to find their passion and ultimately bloom with stunning color.

References

Allen, K. (1996) *Star Shaped Pegs, Square Holes: Nonverbal Learning Disorders and the Growing Up Years.* Livermore: Unicycle Press.

American Psychiatric Association (1994) *Diagnostic and Statistical Manual of Mental Disorders.* Washington, DC: American Psychiatric Association.

Attwood, T. (1998) *Asperger's Syndrome: A Guide for Parents and Professionals.* London: Jessica Kingsley Publishers.

California Health and Human Services Agency (1999) *A Report to the Legislature: Changes in the Population of Persons with Autism and Pervasive Developmental Disorders in California's Developmental Services System: 1987 through 1998.* Sacramento, CA: California Health and Human Services Agency.

Dreikers, R. (1987) *Children: The Challenge.* New York: Plume.

Ehlers, S. and Gillberg, C. (1993) 'The epidemiology of Asperger's Syndrome – A total population study.' *Journal of Child Psychology and Psychiatry 34,* 1327–135.

Frith, U. (ed) (1991) *Autism and Asperger Syndrome.* Cambridge: Cambridge University Press.

Gillberg, C. (1992) 'The Emanuel Miller Memorial Lecture 1991 'Autism and autistic-like conditions: subclasses among disorders of empathy.' *The Journal of Child Psychology and Psychiatry and Allied Disciplines 33,* 5, 813–842.

Grandin, T. (1995) *Thinking in Pictures; and Other Reports from my Life with Autism.* New York: Doubleday.

Gray, C. (1991) *The New Social Stories.* Dallas: Future Horizons, Inc.

Greenspan, S.I. and Weidner, S. (1998) *The Child With Special Needs: Encouraging Intellectual and Emotional Growth.* New York: Perseus Books.

Klin, A., Volkmar, F.R. Sparrow, S.S. (eds) (2000) *Asperger Syndrome.* New York: Guilford Press.

Klin, A., Volkmar, F.R. Sparrow, S. Cicchetti, D.V. and Rourke, B.P. (1995) 'Validity and neuropsychological characterization of Asperger Syndrome: Convergence with nonverbal learning disabilities.' *Journal of Child Psychology and Psychiatry and Allied Disciplines 36,* 7, 1127–1140.

Myles, B.S. and Simpson, R. (1998) *Asperger Syndrome: A Guide for Educators and Parents.* Austin: Pro-Ed, Inc.

Rourke, B.P. (ed) (1995) *Syndrome of Nonverbal Learning Disabilities: Neurodevelopmental Manifestations.* New York: The Guilford Press.

Thompson, S. (1997) *The Source for Nonverbal Learning Disabilities.* Moline: LinguiSystems, Inc.

Volkmar, F.R. *et al.* (1994) DSM-IV Autism/Pervasive Developmental Disorder Field Trial. *American Journal of Psychiatry 151,* 1361–1367.

Wing, L. (1981) 'Asperger's Syndrome: a clinical account.' *Psychological Medicine 11,* 115–130.

WHO (1989) *Tenth Revision of the International Classification of Disease.* Geneva: World Health Organisation.

Websites

ASPEN of America, Inc. (Asperger Syndrome Education Network)
www.asperger.org

NLD On The Web!
www.nldontheweb.org

OASIS (Online Asperger Syndrome Information and Support)
www.udel.edu/bkirby/asperger/